Cacti as House Plants

CACTI AS HOUSE PLANTS

*Flowers of the Desert
in Your Home*

by

W. E. Shewell-Cooper
and
T. C. Rochford

Blandford Press . London

First published in 1973
Copyright © 1973 Blandford Press Ltd.
167 High Holborn, London WC1V 6PH

ISBN 07137 0618 X

Dedication

To Two Horticultural Stalwarts

Lieut.-General Sir Oliver Leese, Bart.
on whose staff Dr. Shewell-Cooper served
during World War II and whose horticultural
interest first started at one of the Command
Horticultural Courses run by Dr. Shewell-Cooper
and
Mr. Tom Rochford, V.M.H.

Printed in Great Britain by
C. Tinling & Co. Ltd., Prescot and London

Colour plates printed by Colour Reproductions Ltd.

Contents

		Page
	List of illustrations	vi
	Preface	viii
1	Introduction and definition	9
2	Flowers, fruit and their uses	12
3	Composts	15
4	The general culture of cacti	18
5	The general culture of other succulents	25
6	Some easy-to-grow cacti and other succulents	30
7	Planting and transplanting	49
8	Seed sowing	52
9	How to take cuttings and graft	58
10	Pests which attack cacti and other succulents	64
11	Fungus diseases	70
12	An extended list of cacti, with descriptions	72
13	A general list of succulents, with descriptions	125
14	Ornamental bowls of succulents	146
	Index	149

List of illustrations

Colour illustrations (nos. 8 to 32) are indicated by bold type.

		Page
1	Cacti and other succulents on a windowsill	29
2	*Cereus peruvianus monstruosus*	
3	*Cephalocereus senilis*	
4	*Astrophytum capricorne aureum*	31
5	*Lobivia famatimensis cristata*	
6	*Gymnocalycium saglione*	
7	*Ferocactus electracanthus*	
8	*Echinocereus fitchii*	33
9	*Aylostera pseudodeminuta*	
10	*Aylostera deminuta*	
11	*Gymnocalycium quehlianum*	34
12	*Gymnocalycium venturianum*	
13	*Gymnocalycium damsii*	
14	*Mammillaria aurihamata*	35
15	*Mammillaria heyderi*	
16	*Mammillaria hahniana*	
17	*Mammillaria rhodantha* var.	36
18	*Mammillaria uncinata*	
19	*Mammillaria zeilmanniana alba*	
20	*Mammillaria zeilmanniana*	
21	*Rebutia (Mediolobivia) pygmaea*	37
22	*Notocactus tabularis*	
23	*Parodia sanguiniflora*	
24	*Parodia gracilis*	38
25	*Parodia microsperma*	
26	*Parodia chrysacanthion*	

27 *Setiechinopsis mirabilis*   39
28 *Pseudolobivia kratochvilleana*
29 *Rhipsalidopsis rosea*
30 Hybrid between *Schlumbergera gaertneri* and
   Rhipsalidopsis rosea   40
31 *Rebutia* hybrid
32 *Rebutia* hybrid
33 *Cereus peruvianus*   59
34 *Opuntia (Brasilopuntia) brasiliensis*
35 *Opuntia leucotricha*
36 *Opuntia* sp.
37 Cacti on display for sale in pots   67
38 *Neobuxbaumia polylopha*
39 *Oreocereus celsianus*
40 *Cleistocactus straussii*   82
41 *Stetsonia coryne*
42 *Gymnocalycium mihanovichii 'hibotan'*
43 *Astrophytum ornatum*
44 *Stenocactus lancifer*   106
45 *Echinocactus grusonii*
46 *Mammillaria microhelia*
47 *Monvillea haagei*

Acknowledgement
All the black and white photographs and nos. 12, 21, 22, 26,
28, 29, 30 and 32 of the colour photographs were taken by
Mr. Milan Svanderlik. The other colour photographs were
taken by Mr. T. C. Rochford

vii

Preface

This book was born in a very unusual manner. T. C. Rochford, who grows over a million cacti for sale each year as part of his family's extensive pot plant industry, developed his first interest in cacti at the age of 9 years. In fact, he built up a cactus collection as the result of Dr. W. E. Shewell-Cooper's first book on cacti and succulents which he bought in the 1950s.

These two never met until 1970 when Rochford's held a large party in order to show to the Press the thousands of different flowering cacti they were growing, which they called 'Flowers from the Desert'.

The result of this effort was a tentative enquiry from Dr. Shewell-Cooper to Thomas Rochford IV as to whether an authoritative work could be written which would prove of help to beginners all over the world who wanted to grow cacti successfully. Thus the student became master to the professor!

Thomas Rochford IV, who grows large numbers of cacti and also imports them for distribution all over England, is in a unique position to know which varieties are commonly met with in stores and shops and he is sympathetically aware of the problems of identification.

Throughout the book the two authors have aimed to give clear guidance to a beginner with no botanical knowledge, and also to instil a certain amount of this in the course of reading the book.

Dr. Shewell-Cooper stayed many weeks in Bordighera, Italy, where he was entertained by the Cactus Growers' Association. He was helped particularly by Cavaliere Lodovico Ronco, who spent days with him going round to see the various cactus growers and explaining [in excellent French] all the intricacies of cactus growing. It is marvellous to be able to see these fascinating plants—most of them out of doors—in a land which seems paradise to them.

This book is not intended to be a complete work on the subject of cacti and succulents. It is an amateur's book dealing with the growing of these plants and it is hoped that it will therefore be of value to the hundreds of amateurs throughout the country.

We must thank Mr. Michael Gibson (who at one time was the Head Student of the Horticultural Training College, Arkley) for his help in producing the book and our thanks must also go to Mrs. Moody and Mrs. Pat Clarke who have typed the whole of this script very expertly and patiently.

The International Horticultural Advisory Bureau,   W. E. Shewell-Cooper
Arkley, S. Herts
                                                        T. C. Rochford

I

Introduction and definition

It can be said with truth that all cacti are succulents but that all succulents are not cacti. The main characteristic of a succulent is the fact that it has either an extremely fleshy stem or very fleshy leaves, or even both. The succulents are found in the deserts of the world. Most of them grow directly on the sand or soil but some will 'squat' on other plants, usually trees, but not as parasites, for they have the ability of abstracting the sustenance they need from the air.

They are mostly found in the Americas and even in the prairies of Canada; hundreds, for instance, are to be discovered in Mexico and lower California. Some may be found growing naturally in Alaska. Friends have seen them just as happy in Patagonia. They are well known in Peru and Chile.

In Africa they are found in Eritrea, Somalia and Abyssinia. In Australia they are seen in the Sand Plains though they are not necessarily indigenous. The writers have seen them in the Canary Islands, in German South West Africa (as it then was), on the Karoo in South Africa and in Cape Province proper. It is here that the Aloes and Euphorbias do so well and grow surprisingly large in the open. As one might imagine, it is *Euphorbia canariensis* which flourishes in the Canary Isles, as do many species of the Crassulaceae.

The great function, of course, of the fleshy foliage is that it is able to hold moisture during the very long hot periods of sun. A plant that has to grow in an open dry situation needs to be fashioned in this way. Because the plants come on the whole from the hot arid regions, very few of them are absolutely hardy in Britain and countries with a similar climate, where they have to be given some protection during the winter. Some plants, as will be seen in chapters 12 and 13, need quite high temperatures if they are to do well. Most specimens are grown in greenhouses, but there are many types which can live quite happily in the house.

When plants normally live under tropical conditions, or in arid areas, they undergo particularly curious climatic conditions. They may, for instance, be baked almost dry by the hottest of hot suns for months at a time, and then suddenly they will be plunged into a period of torrential rains, with heat at the same time. The result is that during the dry periods the plants make little or no growth and during the torrents they not only try to increase in size, but they flower and fruit as well. This gives the key for the suggested treatment of cacti and succulents in chapters 4 and 5.

With cacti and succulents which have no leaves, there is as a result a minimum of transpiration. This is similar to perspiration in human beings. Most cacti have spines or thorns instead of leaves.

All succulents (including cacti) produce flowers and sometimes quite showy ones. As Sir Oliver Leese said in his famous lecture in the Royal Horticultural Society Hall, 'One of the phenomena of this weird land is the strange shapes of the plants which, whilst bearing little resemblance to other flower-bearing plants in the world to-day, produce these lovely flowers. Their unknown ancestors, after centuries of existence in a region becoming progressively drier, reduced their branches and twigs to spines—and either diminished these leaves to all but invisible scales or discarded them altogether for spines—with the skin of the plant producing chlorophyll and transferring the function of food manufacture from the leaf to the trunk and stems of the plant.'

Another interesting point is that cacti, unlike other plants, have aeroles, which produce spines, and new joints which root when they fall to the ground or are transplanted. These areoles are in fact the vital growing areas of cacti.

The photographs of cacti give a very clear idea as to what these plants are like. Many of them are round. Nearly all of them are covered by quite a thick skin which has very few breathing pores. In some cases the spines or thorns are long and beautiful. In other cases the spines are formed amongst long white hairs. The cacti belong to the family Cactaceae. Actually, there are more than 2,000 different species. Botanists divide these up into 3 main tribes: (1) Pereskieae, (2) Opuntieae and (3) Cereeae. This third tribe is divided into 8 subtribes, details of which will be found in chapter 8.

The succulents are to be found in many different families. Agaves, for instance, belong to the Amaryllidaceae, *Bryophyllum* to the family Crassulaceae, Euphorbias to Euphorbiaceae and Mesembryanthemums to the Azoiaceae family. The word 'succulent' is a general term used by the gardener and not really recognised by the true botanist. Whereas cacti have their own separate family, other succulents may, and in fact do, come from different families.

In order to get hold of the water they need, some plants (and this is particularly true in the case of succulents) will send down their roots very deep indeed. On the other hand, there are many species which have very shallow fibrous roots and so are able to absorb very quickly the dew which may fall in the evening hours. In the desert, of course, the surface soil is not disturbed by a gardener hoeing—and the result is the root hairs can come right up to the surface of the ground in their desire to pick up any dew that may fall. Some succulents may look absolutely dried up and shrunken during the resting period, that is to say during the months when they receive no water. Others take the precaution of bearing their leaves in a rosette form (this again is more typical of the succulents than the cacti) and this rosette may then close up tightly in the hottest sunshine and thus reduce transpiration as well as giving protection.

The strong spines (or thorns) on many species of cacti are there to give protection from feeding animals. They also help by deflecting the sun's rays. They encourage the collection of moisture; they also provide shade, particularly so in the case of the very hairy plants. Some succulents have stems similar to some true cacti, for instance the genus *Stapelia*. This genus produces star-fish like flowers which emit a carrion-like odour in order to attract flies and thus ensure pollination.

With both succulents and cacti it is best not to shade, except in the case of the epiphytic plants, but it is advisable to ensure adequate ventilation during the hottest and sunniest periods of the year. In the countries where they come from, they usually live right out in the open and on the whole they love the sunny spots, though in the Karoo (South Africa) you will find Stapeliads, Gasterias and Haworthias under bushes. They grow in situations which are perfectly drained and therefore they hate anything like impeded drainage when growing in pots or even in borders in the greenhouse. It is when the drainage is perfect that cacti will grow in the same pot for 4–5 years without being disturbed at all—but the plants will never grow larger.

The late Mr. W. W. Pettigrew, V.M.H., the Park Superintendent of Manchester, whom Dr. Shewell-Cooper followed as gardening broadcaster at the North Regional BBC, used to use rainwater for his cacti because he was worried about 'chalk' in the tap water. He gave his plants a complete rest from October to April and during that time they were not watered at all. At the first watering in the spring he gave a thorough soaking. Today many experts prefer a resting period from mid-November to the end of February only.

His exception to the rule was in the case of the epiphytal cacti (those are the cacti, as already mentioned, which normally—within natural habitat—get their moisture out of the air) and here a certain amount of water had to be applied even in the depth of winter. Such cacti usually require a higher temperature and, though perhaps more suited for greenhouse culture, can be grown in the house.

2

Flowers, fruit and their uses

It is not only that cacti and succulents are interesting; they can be very decorative as well. Many of them bear the most beautiful flowers. We have seen, for instance, the Prickly Pears (*Opuntia*) in bloom and they bear large, yellow flowers which are very attractive indeed. The Hedgehog Cactus (*Echinocereus*) as its name suggests, is covered all over with strong spines, but the flowers are an orange-red with a glorious yellow centre. The Giant Cacti of the Arizona Desert, commonly called by Americans Saguaro or Sahuaio (botanically *Carnegiea*), bears huge yellowy-white flowers with a yellow centre to them and these are so outstanding that the State of Arizona has adopted them as their emblem, just as the rose is the emblem for England.

The flower colours in cacti vary from dark crimson to violet, from orange to pink and red, from yellow to dark crimson and from white to purple. Most of the flowers have a beautiful metallic sheen. Many of the finest blooms are born at night time. The flowers open out in all their glory at the setting of the sun, they are at their best perhaps at midnight and by dawn they have passed away again. The flowers of some cacti, however, are at their best for two days. Others may be in flower for five days; some during this short period open up fully in the daytime and then close their blooms at nightfall. A few, like those of the *Echinopsis*, are beautifully perfumed. Some succulents, such as the *Stapelia*, stink to high heaven!

Don't believe the so-called local expert who will tell you that cacti will only flower once every seven years. There is no truth in this at all. There are plants which bloom every season, sometimes several times in a season, even under what might be called the least ideal conditions. It is important, if one expects flowering, to carry out the general culture given in chapter 4 in all its detail. For instance, plants must be allowed to rest throughout the winter; the temperature must never drop below 5° C (40° F). During the winter months never allow them suddenly to have any extra heat or they will, so to speak, wake up and start to do things they shouldn't do! Always see that the plants have plenty of air—and by that we mean fresh air.

Be prepared to water quite freely in the summer. See that the plants are grown in the right compost, as advised in chapter 3, and then when it comes to October start to reduce the watering. Buy plants that have not been grown too rapidly. There are always some unscrupulous suppliers who want to get rich quickly and who produce a forced cactus plant; one that has been given perhaps too much water and too much heat. Such a plant is not likely to flower. It is far more likely to die.

Go to a reliable nurseryman, tell him that you want good plants that are likely to flower and trust him to sell you the right species. We can well recommend the following: *Chamascereus silvestrii, Gymnocalycium damsii, Gymnocalycium quehlianum, Mammillaria bocasana, Mammillaria kewensis, Mammillaria prolifera, Rebutia minuscula, Zygocactus truncatus* and *Notocactus concinnus*.

The flowers are, of course, followed by fruits, and these are usually one-celled berries in cacti. In many cases the fruits are edible. We do not know of one case in which they may be said to be poisonous. Abroad, again and again, Dr. Shewell-Cooper has eaten and enjoyed the fruits of the Prickly Pear, whose Latin name is *Opuntia ficus-indica*. On a hot day these pears can be very refreshing indeed. The great thing is to get somebody else to peel them if possible because the skins are covered with very fine hairy spines or prickles and these, when they get into your skin, are very difficult to get out. There are some species of *Opuntia* which are specifically cultivated for their fruits.

We are told that the lovely red fruits of some of the Mammillarias are delicious to eat, having a strawberry-like flavour. There are similar red fruits of Epiphyllums which are pleasant to eat, though they are diuretic. The Mexicans eat berries which are shaped very much like olives and of a bluish shade, picked from a species of *Myrtillocactus*. They call them Garambullos.

In tropical countries some of the Opuntias are used as green fodder for cattle. The natives scorch the outsides over an open fire in order to burn off the spines.

Another Mexican custom was to use the *Lophophora williamsii* as a kind of drug. Evidently when the tops of this cacti were dried and were then cooked and eaten, they had a tremendously exhilarating effect, something like cocaine. This was due to the alkaloids in the tissues of the plant. We understand, however, that the eating of this particular form of cacti is now prohibited.

In South Africa, Euphorbias are used as fodder and in fact the old Boers called *Euphorbia hamata*, 'Beeskragg', which means the strength of an ox.

After their beasts had been pulling for some time and were tired, they used to give them some of these *Euphorbia* to eat and soon afterwards they were able to work and pull as strongly as before. Sometimes natives dig up succulents because they find the roots watery and thirst quenching. This is true, for instance, of the *Fochea damarana*. Another species of *Fochea* is used in some parts of South Africa as a vegetable. The tuber of the *Testudinaria* which is so good and rich is known to the natives as Hottentot Bread, because of the starch it contains. The tubers have been imported for the extraction of cortisone.

Many times as a boy in South Africa Dr. Shewell-Cooper has eaten the Kaffir figs, which are the fruits of the *Carpobrotus edulis*; the plants are also often used to prevent soil erosion. The flowers are beautiful and the fruits quite tasty. The *Agave sisalana* gives the sisal hemp which is much used by manufacturers today. Another succulent, *Euphorbia dregeana*, contains about 70 per cent. resin and about 18 per cent. rubber and for this reason it is sometimes cultivated in South Africa for the rubber content.

One can go on talking about the uses of succulents; for example there is a Mexican Agave which produces a very popular alcoholic drink known as Pulque. There are species of Aloes which contain resins that can be used medicinally. There is a *Euphorbia* which produces gum used by veterinary surgeons. Many other Euphorbias are used as hedging plants because of their thorns. This is more common in South Africa than elsewhere.

3

Composts

The word compost may mean two things: (a) a special mixture of soil in which it is suitable to grow plants in pots and pots and boxes, or (b) a heap of vegetable waste, which is purposely being activated by fish manure or the like so as to produce bulky organic matter for the garden. Thanks to the work done by the John Innes Horticultural Institution, it has been possible to standardise the compost used for the great majority of plants in the greenhouse.

As far as cacti and succulents are concerned, the gardener should aim at producing a compost which will be very open and porous. It is inadvisable to use a heavy clay soil, for instance, and growers who have had such a soil in their gardens and have had to use it have baked the clay first to ensure that it loses its stickiness. One can make up a compost with the ordinary soil of the garden and mix it with an equal part of really coarse silver sand, adding to each 6-in. (15 cm) potful a ½ teaspoonful of carbonate of lime.

Another compost which has been used with great success consists of 1 part ordinary garden soil, 1 part coarse silver sand and 1 part sedge peat, adding ½ teaspoonful of carbonate of lime to each 6-in. (15 cm) potful. Some have recommended the use of charcoal, but the authors have not found this necessary. The use of sedge peat is particularly important in the case of the epiphytic types of cacti; they like such material because it will help to hold water.

As drainage is so important, it is a very good idea when using soil to use a very fine sieve—say ⅛ in. (0·3 cm)—so as to sift out all the dust. Otherwise there is a danger that this may seep down to the crocks below and so cause impeded drainage. A good form of lime for cacti consists of dried egg shells. These can always be crushed finely before they are used. The sand in the compost must always be coarse because this will help to keep the compost open and so allow the air to circulate around the roots. Some growers are against the use of lime for cacti, but the authors have used it very successfully.

John Innes Potting Compost No. 1 has proved very satisfactory for cacti and other succulents, with slight modifications. It consists of 7 parts bulk medium loam, 3 parts bulk sedge peat and 2 parts bulk coarse sand. You add to each bushel of this mixture (or pro rata) 1 oz (28 gms) ground limestone, 1½ oz (42 gms) hoof and horn meal and 1½ oz superphosphate. The soil should be sterilized before being used and should be passed through a ½-in. (1·3 cm) sieve to be in the right condition.

The modifications suggested for cacti consist of the addition of an extra part of coarse sand and an extra ½ part of sedge peat. The feeds may then be reduced to 1 oz (28 gms) hoof and horn, 1 oz superphosphate and ½ oz (14 gms) sulphate of potash plus the usual 1 oz (28 gms) ground limestone. The value of using just a little fertiliser is that the plants do not suffer from lack of food even though the roots are confined into a small pot. In order to obtain good flowers and good seeds to follow some food must be supplied so that the plant growth is not retarded. The alternative to using food is continually to re-pot or to take off the top ½ in. (1·3 cm) of soil and replace this with compost. Start with the modified John Innes Compost as above and all should be well for at least two years.

If there are any definite exceptions the authors have tried to give them when describing the individual species of cacti. The important thing is not to overdo any plant food, because you do not want soft growth, and to be particularly careful with the desert types of cacti because these really do not like organic fertilisers.

When the compost is made up, it should be just moist. That is to say, if it is squeezed in the hand no water should emerge, and yet when the hand is open the portion of soil should retain its shape and should not fall apart until it is lightly touched. Just a word of warning against the use of leaf mould: it is sometimes full of weed seeds and fungus diseases and also unfortunately often harbours insects. By the way, the lime bought should always be carbonate of lime and not a hydrated lime. Some gardeners can get hold of lime and mortar from old buildings; this is very useful. Others living by the sea crush shells and find this first-class.

Never be liberal with liquid manures, and be careful when buying the sand; it should not come from the sea shore because the salt will not be helpful. Furthermore, salt always attracts moisture and a salty compost would be too wet for cacti. Plants grown in a saline compost invariably rot off at the roots.

For those who have difficulties in obtaining soil because of living in flats, it is nice to know that it is possible to buy a John Innes Cactus Compost already prepared. Besides this some horticultural sundriesmen will make up the additions at source and supply the amateur with the exact compost he needs.

Seed compost
Those who are raising plants from seed will need to make up a compost consisting of 2 parts sterilised loam, 1 part sedge peat, 1 part coarse silver sand and 1 part crushed brick. (One cannot over-emphasise the importance of the coarseness of the sand particles.) The loam or soil should be sterilised. This means heating it to a temperature of 100°C (212°F) and keeping it at this temperature for 10 minutes before allowing it to cool down. It is possible to buy soil from a good nurseryman or horticultural sundriesman. (Make sure, however, that this has been sterilised.) Mix in with each 6-in. (15 cm) potful of this compost a teaspoonful of carbonate of lime.

A method of sterilising soil at home is to put a small quantity in a biscuit tin in an oven. Large quantities may be sterilised by filling a large bucket full of soil and hanging it from a cross-bar into a copper of boiling water in such a manner that the water cannot boil over into the bucket. The object, just to remind you, is to get the soil heated to 100°C (212°F) and to keep it at this temperature for 10 minutes. It is advisable, therefore, to immerse a reliable thermometer into the centre of the soil about 3 in. (7·6 cm) down so as to be certain of results. A rough guide can be made if a potato the size of a hen's egg is buried 1 in. (2·5 cm) down in the bucket. When this is cooked the soil will have been properly treated.

Those who do not wish to sterilise will be well advised to water the soil with a solution of Potassium oxy-quinoline sulphate. One part of this should be dissolved in two thousand parts of water. Your local chemist will be able to help you by making up a solution and by telling you how to dilute it.

A succulent compost
Those who are dealing with succulents only may like to know of a compost which has proved very useful at the time when the seedlings are pricked out. In these conditions it is advisable to use a slightly richer mixture and thus the compost consists of 3 parts sterilised soil, 2 parts sedge peat, $\frac{1}{2}$ part brick dust or mortar rubble, 3 parts sharp silver sand with coarse particles. If it is impossible to get mortar rubble or brick dust, fine fully consumed ashes may be used plus a teaspoonful of carbonate of lime to each 6-in. (15 cm) potful prepared. This compost must be well mixed together and be passed through a $\frac{1}{4}$-in. (0·6 cm) sieve before being used.

4

The general culture of cacti

As gardeners the authors find it particularly difficult to generalise. It must be equally difficult for a child psychologist to generalise on 'bringing up young people'. Every child is different, as parents well know, and has to be treated differently. But there are certain rules which apply to all children, just as there are definite instructions which apply to almost all cacti. Remember then that the suggestions made in this chapter are of a general character and so for any special needs, turn to chapter 12.

Principal requirements

Cacti as a whole ask for three things: sunshine, light and air. It may seem peculiar to include the sun as well as light, but as the Bible reveals quite clearly in Genesis I they are two quite different things. There is something more in the sun's rays than just the light produced, and the cacti need both. They like to grow, for instance, in a place where there is plenty of reflected light. They prefer rooms where the walls are light in colour or even white, rather than rooms where there is very dark wallpaper.

This is one of the reasons why cacti do so well in a greenhouse. There the woodwork is painted white (or should be), there the rays of the sun are impeded as little as possible, and there it is possible to ventilate whenever it is desired. The greenhouse should always be in a sunny, open place. If it is convenient, the house, however small, should run north and south; a span roof type of house is always best.

It is not essential to have a special greenhouse for cacti and succulents only. They can be grown on the shelving of a house that is used for other flowering plants. The shelf should be high up and near the glass so that the plants get the maximum amount of sunshine and will never receive the drip from other plants when watering.

Having said these things, it must be realised that cacti are plants which can be badly treated and yet go on growing and giving pleasure to their owners month after month. There are no plants which survive bad-handling better than the cacti. Mis-use them and they will still come up smiling. Fail to water them, and instead of dying, they will persist. Leave them in the same pots for years, and they will do their best. Perhaps the only time that they really do object is when overwatering is done and the soil is sodden. That is the reason they should *never* be stood in saucers of water—a habit which is common, unfortunately, in some homes.

In the home

It is when one becomes bitten with the fascination of growing cacti and succulents that a little greenhouse becomes necessary. Until then it is possible to start with a small collection in the home. Cacti do quite well in a living-room, but here they are always best if kept on the window sill, where they can get the maximum of light and sunshine and, of course, air too. The only exception to this rule, perhaps, is in the frostiest periods of the year, when it may pay to remove the plants from the window sill at night time and replace them there early in the morning.

Don't keep your cacti on the mantelpiece, where they may look decorative, but where they will suffer from lack of sun and light and, in addition, where they may have to put up with the extra heat of a fire below. It is possible to-day to buy miniature greenhouses, say 2 ft (61 cm) long by about 1 ft (30·5 cm) wide, in order to grow the cacti in these on the window sill. The disadvantage of such a system is that some of the sunlight is kept off and some of the sun's rays may be kept out. The advantages are that the plants do not get covered with dust and they are protected from draughts.

One can choose the sunny south window for the types which have strong spines and white spines, but in the case of the spineless species, which tend to be light green in colour, they should be placed in a north window for they like a slightly shadier position. Those who have centrally heated houses must take care not to allow the plants to be overwarm in the winter time, since, because of the lack of sunshine, the plants may grow weak and spindly. It might be possible to have the plants for this reason in, say, a spare room which was not centrally heated and thus allow the cacti to have their normal winter's rest.

Water and watering

Generally speaking, under the conditions in which cacti grow abroad, they either obtain their water from very heavy dews, which seem to collect on the spines and trickle down to the roots, or they rely on tremendous torrential drenches which soak the soil thoroughly. The roots, which seem to be all over the place, even up to the surface of the ground, then take up the moisture in large quantities and store it in the fleshy body or leaves of the plant.

Many cacti like to grow close to large rock formations and then it would seem the roots are able to penetrate into moist, cool crevices and even right down to the base of the rocks, where there may be water even in small quantities. The plant then itself may be in full sun and the roots in moist shade. These things are said because they provide a clue to what the gardener has to do for his plants when he is growing them in pots in the home or greenhouse.

It can be said that when plants are being grown under the ideal conditions of a well-ventilated bright greenhouse there should be no need to water at all from the beginning of October to, say, the beginning of March. In sunny years it may be necessary to go on watering until the end of October, while those who live in the Worthing area, in the south of England, which is famous for its sunshine, may have to start watering again in February instead of in March. Bearing these variations in mind, divide the year into two periods; the spring and summer, when water is given, and the resting period when no watering is done.

There are exceptions to every rule. When plants are growing in the house, for instance, it is often advisable owing to the dryness of the atmosphere caused by central heating or electric fires (or worse still gas fires) to continue to give water once a month. Another exception concerns the Epiphyllums, which seem to need water every month of the year with the exception, say, of the two months after flowering.

When one changes over from the no watering period to the watering régime, it is necessary to start gradually. The soil having been allowed to get really dry will not easily absorb water. This will tend either to 'float' on the surface of the soil, or trickle down the air space around the edge of the pot and so get away without moistening the ball of earth. One always starts by giving moderate quantities of water so that by the end of four weeks the plants are used to receiving moisture and can be watered in the normal way.

At the end of the period, one wants to reduce the regularity of the watering gradually also. It is never advisable to withhold water suddenly. The plan is just to give less for the next few weeks so that the time may come in the greenhouse when no water is given at all. If the soil at the top of the pot tends to get caked because of overhead watering, then it must be disturbed a little so that the moisture can get through. It always helps, of course, when potting up if the soil is not higher than say $\frac{1}{4}$ in. (0·6 cm) from the top of the pot so that there is always a 'catchment area' in which the water may be held prior to it seeping down through the compost.

There are excellent little watering cans made by Haws, which have a nice curved spout and it is easy to use these for filling up the little cacti pots when this becomes necessary. It is better to do this than to employ a larger can and so have to pour water over the plants. This does not mean to say that cacti need never be syringed over. They do like a wash now and then. One should not, however, syringe when the sun is shining on the plants, for then drops of water may act like a magnifying glass and cause the skin of the cactus to burn and thus a mark is left plus a wound, which may allow the entry of disease.

Try to water early in the morning, then one may be fairly certain that all the unnecessary moisture will have evaporated by night time. In a very hot summer, and under droughty conditions, some gardeners like to water in the evening just after the sun has gone to bed. The tendency then is for the humid atmosphere to produce artificial dew on the cacti and they will appreciate this. Never, however, water in the evening after a dull day or even when it is feared that the following day may be dull.

Though it has been stated by one of the British research stations that it is possible to water plants in the greenhouse with water direct from the tap, undoubtedly it pays to use rain water if possible with cacti and to make certain that the water is at the same temperature as the house. For this reason it is a good idea to put a bucket of water into the greenhouse in the evening, so that by the morning it is at the same temperature as the soil in the pots.

Far more harm occurs through over-watering than from under-watering and, therefore, a good rule is : if in doubt—don't! In the summer the aim should be to give a nice soaking once a week for the small plants (more frequently if in very tiny pots which dry out quickly) and with the larger specimens it may be necessary to increase the dose to once a day during the months of June, July and August. Even then one has to reduce the dosage to, say, twice a week after the middle of August, and once a week in early September.

One should remember that on the whole the globe-shaped plants need less water than the taller-growing types. It should also be borne in mind that plants in rooms generally require more moisture than plants in a greenhouse. Watch the plants carefully and if there is any sign of shrivelling, then a watering is necessary, for the shrivelling shows that the plant is living on its reserves.

One of the best methods of watering is by dipping rather than applying the moisture from above. This can be done by standing a number of pots in a sieve or tray and then dipping them in a bowl of tepid rain water. When doing this care must be taken to ensure that the pot ball is thoroughly soaked. Naturally one needs to have the same size of pots in the container at one time. The reason that people do not adopt this dipping method when they have large numbers of plants is that it takes too long to do.

Clean glass

It is extremely important to make certain that the glass of the greenhouse or the window is absolutely clean, especially in towns and cities. Greasy or sooty deposits will soon foul glass with the result that it is never clean even when washed by the rain. One can do much by washing the glass over outside with a good detergent in water. In northern towns and cities this work may have to be done once a month. In cases where the glass is really grimy, it is advisable to wash down with a strong acid, such as Premex, and having applied this over the glass, it has to be washed off a minute later before it etches into the surface.

Don't forget that if you happen to have the gutters of the greenhouse connected to an inside tank (and some do this to collect the rainwater) you must put a plug in the downspout to prevent the acid from running in. This applies also when you use the detergent. Incidentally, it is a good practice to wash the glass inside once a year. In fact, everything should be done to allow the maximum of sunlight and sun rays to penetrate through the glass.

Heating

When cacti are kept in the home, they have to put up with whatever temperature the room rises to during the day. Curiously enough, rooms are often hotter in the winter than in the summer, owing to electrical heating or a good roaring fire. It is then that cactus plants will appreciate being as near the window as possible and, in consequence, far away from the fire. Of course, at night time the temperature drops considerably and the plants can be moved into the centre of the room, or they may be left where they are provided there is a thick curtain between them and the glass window.

At a horticultural training centre, the greenhouse in which the cacti are kept is heated by gas, with the result that it is possible to keep the plants at a definite temperature almost all the year round. In such a case the thermostat which controls the temperature should be set at $7°C$ ($45°F$).

Oddly enough, it doesn't matter if the temperature of the house rises quite high in the summer months if this rise is due to sun heat and not to artificial heat. At a temperature of $7°$ to $10°C$ ($45°$ to $50°F$) gas heating does not work out too expensive. The Gas Council have introduced a very useful gas heater.

It is possible to heat a greenhouse by means of a paraffin stove, but it is important to buy the special types made for this purpose and then to take every precaution to see that no poisonous fumes are given off. One always has to keep the wicks in perfect condition for the sooty carbon must never be allowed to be deposited on the cacti. One can heat a house by means of hot water pipes and the right type of stove and in some areas it is possible to use gas for heating the water instead of anthracite or coke. The problem of using the hard fuel is that with the very small boilers it is necessary to stoke them as late as midnight under hard, frosty conditions.

In a state of emergency such as the heat failing always plan to cover the plants up with several sheets of newspaper, for this will give some protection and prevent excessive radiation of heat from the plants and the soil. This keeping in of the heat by means of newspaper will prevent damage by two or three degrees of frost, especially if the newspaper is not removed until about 11 o'clock in the morning. It is always a bad thing to allow the sun to strike first thing in the morning on plants that have been 'touched' by the frost during the night.

Generally speaking, if the temperature is kept above say 3°C (38°F) all will be well. It is not that plants cannot stand frost; some of them have to put up with this in their own countries, but there the atmosphere is absolutely dry and so they do not suffer. In the greenhouse in Britain you invariably get a damp type of frost and it is that which is fatal to the cacti. The only exceptions to the rule are the really tropical succulents, especially those that come from Madagascar which like a high night temperature; but even then it need not be higher than 10°C (50°F).

Ventilation

Ventilation is nothing but fresh air. Plants breathe as human beings do, but in a somewhat different way, and need a fresh supply of air all the time. See to it, therefore, that the cacti do not grow in a fuggy atmosphere. Don't have them too close together; give them breathing space. In the summer it should be possible to keep the windows open all the time. See to it that the air enters naturally and that the foetid atmosphere gets out. Do not allow any draughts.

In the winter the windows or ventilators should be opened whenever the temperature inside the house rises above 10°C (50°F). However, they must be closed during fog and rain whatever the temperature and only opened up afterwards to clear any humidity inside the house.

Good flowering is dependent on ripening of the flowering areas on the plants and this is achieved in winter by maintaining plants in a cool dry situation. If possible it is best to ventilate a cactus greenhouse by means of a fan since this maintains an efficient air circulation. During winter condensation frequently builds up in the evenings on the inside of the glass; it is a good idea to open the ventilators or switch on the fan for a quarter of an hour before sunset in order to clear this.

So keen are the plants on good circulation of fresh air—for remember that they grow in regions where there is no pollution by factory chimneys—that some cactus growers like to put their precious specimens out on shelving which is actually fitted *outside* the window sills. Here they must be fixed in such a way that they cannot topple down to the street below. Where there is plenty of fresh air, there are seldom serious diseases or pests.

The disadvantage of growing plants in the open is that they may be damaged by rain and wind. That is one of the reasons why they are not usually planted out of doors. Some have got over the difficulty of growing them in the open by covering them with the square sectional glass frames known as access frames. These flat-topped 'cloches' give protection against wind and rain and yet provide the maximum ventilation almost automatically. They enable the cactus grower to put out large numbers of his plants into the open for the summer and this enables him to clean his greenhouse or to use it for some purpose, such as growing tomatoes during the warmer months. It is during this 'removal' period that the glass can be washed down properly.

Staking

It is very seldom that cacti need staking, for most types are nice and firm and stand up on their own. If there are any tall types which are tending to topple over, it is convenient to use a thin stick shaped to the size of a bamboo, which has been dipped in Rentokil and so is green in colour and unobtrusive. The tie around the cactus itself must never be tight, or else when growth develops the string will cut into the skin. The soft green twist that is sold by most horticultural sundriesmen is suitable. If a 'clove hitch' is made around the bamboo, it will prevent it from rising or falling and so keep it in the exact position made.

Drips

Never allow any holes or cracks in your greenhouse or water may drip on to the plants and this is fatal. The cactus growers' rule must be 'no drips'!

5

The general culture of other succulents

The general culture and care of other succulents is naturally very similar indeed to that of cacti. In fact it can be said that those who can look after a cactus successfully should have no difficulty in caring for other succulents. On the whole, the compost can be slightly richer and in addition it is a useful thing for it to be somewhat coarser. With types like the *Mesembryanthemums*, for instance, it is necessary when making up the John Innes Potting Compost 1 to add double the amount of coarse silver sand.

Principal requirements
The great majority of the other succulents come from hot countries and that means that they are best grown in an adequately heated greenhouse similar to that advised for cacti, but most are quite successful when used as room plants. The ideal method for a succulent would be to grow it on in the greenhouse and then, when it is just about to flower, bring it into the home where it will look particularly decorative. It can remain there for a number of weeks and then, when flowering is over, it can go back into the greenhouse again.

In the greenhouse it is necessary to be able to shade during the hottest and sunniest months of the year. It is possible to buy what is called 'Summer Cloud'. This is green in colour and, when mixed with water, can be sprayed on to the glass in such a way that it will break up the sun's rays and so prevent any scorching taking place. Such shade may be only necessary in the case of plants which want special care.

It is quite a good idea to have a 6-in. (15 cm) layer of washed gravel or Lytag on the staging of the house and then to sink the pots into this. The result is that if the edges of the pots are hidden with small stones, the plants look as if they are growing naturally in the gravel itself. Some types of succulents look themselves like little stones and these are particularly attractive when growing among brownish pebbles. The *Dinteranthus* have a pebbly look about them also and are in what may be called their natural habitat when growing in and among rough limestone.

This plunging of the plants does, of course, prevent the excessive drying out of moisture from the sides of the containers and gives protection to the roots from the sun. It is difficult also to over-water under such conditions for the drainage below is so good.

In the house

It is important when succulents are in the house to see that they have plenty of light and air. The drainage must be perfect also. There are, of course, many different kinds of succulents and it is difficult, therefore, to be even as dictatorial about them as it was in the case of cacti in the previous chapter. On the whole they have to be kept dry for some part of the year. For this reason they dislike being in a kitchen where there may be steam from a kettle or from a saucepan on the boil.

Aim with most succulents, as has already been said, to have the plants in for a certain number of weeks in the year, when they are at their best, and then see that they go back into the greenhouse where they can have better conditions and thus a longer life can be ensured.

Water and watering

Most of the succulents should be given a fair amount of water in the summer. They ought to see the watering can once a week. In the winter, however, they will only want water once a month, though with the Echeverias, watering twice or three times every three weeks may be necessary. Aloes may be watered once every three weeks.

The general rules with regard to watering as given for cacti on page 20 apply to other succulents. It must be remembered that because of their construction the plants can store food either in the root or stem. Many East African and Madagascan plants which are becoming popular need a winter temperature of $12°C$ to $15°C$ ($55°$ to $60°F$).

There are perhaps two types which may be described as exceptions to the rule. The first are the Conophytums, which should be given no water from the beginning of May to the end of July. During this period the plants should dry up completely and they will look quite dead. They are, however, producing nice fresh growth underneath their dead looking covering and this eventually will split off and reveal the new plant early in the autumn. It is shortly after this that the flowers are seen.

The second are the Lithops, which always look like little pebbles on the ground; they need complete rest from Boxing Day until the beginning of May. They, so to speak, live on their own 'fat', the moisture from the old feeding the new little stone-like growth which will appear. It is a crime, therefore, to water them in January, February, March and April.

Echeverias seem to like watering about once a week in the winter, especially if the temperature of the house is kept round about 15°C (60°F). Euphorbias, on the other hand, should be given very little water in the winter. Try to learn something about the resting periods of the plants you are growing because though most of them rest in the winter, there are some which behave quite differently. The *Conophytums* have their resting period in the spring and early summer. The *Dactylopsis* and the *Nananthus* do most of their growing in the winter in Great Britain and rest during the summer. The *Cheiridopsis* do the bulk of their growing from the middle of August to the third or fourth week of December.

The nurseryman from whom the plants are bought is usually an expert on the subject and can give his customer the necessary information. It is quite a good thing to have on the label giving the name of the plant, some indication as to the resting months. It is a simple thing, for instance, to put the words, '11 to 5' or '6 to 9' meaning, of course, the 11th to 5th months or the 6th to 9th months. Thus the owner of a collection knows immediately how the particular plant has to be treated while his curious friends have no idea what the mystic symbols represent. This is a great help when other members of the family have to do the watering while, say father, the real expert, is away.

Heating

As a general rule succulents grow well at a temperature of about 17°C (55°F) in the summer months and they will not suffer if the temperature does not fall lower than 7°C (45°F) in the winter. In practice, the temperature may fall as low as 5°C (40°F) at night time without any harm being done, and this is especially true if the plants are kept on the dry side.

Ventilation

Be sure to give plenty of fresh air to succulents in exactly the same way as advised for cacti on page 23.

Staking

Some of the taller types of succulents may need some support. It is convenient to use a thin sliver of wood that has been dyed green by being dipped in Rentokil. This will not only be unobtrusive, but it will also last longer because the Rentokil will prevent it being attacked by fungus diseases. Tie the branches of whatever succulent needs support to the thin stake by means of green twist or twill.

Among the succulents that need some support are *Crassula*, *Kalanchoe*, *Bryophyllum* and *Gasteria*, when in flower.

Special pots

When one becomes really expert on the subject of succulents, it is soon realised that the normal plant pots are not quite as suitable as they are, say, for Fuchsias or Geraniums. For instance, if one is growing succulents that are very shallow rooters such as Stapelias, then it pays to grow in a moderately shallow pan which may be 8 in. (20·3 cm) across and only 4 or 5 in. (10·2 to 12·7 cm) deep. On the other hand, where the plants have long tap roots, like many of the *Lithops* and *Nananthus*, the pots must be deep, say 7 in. (17·8 cm) wide and 5 in. (12·7 cm) deep or 6 in. (15 cm) wide and 4 in. (10·2 cm) deep, and pro rata.

There are Euphorbias, and particularly the club-shaped ones, which need very deep pots indeed, say 5 in. (12·7 cm) wide and 5½ in. (13·9 cm) deep, or 4 in. (10·2 cm) wide and 4½ in. (11·4 cm) deep. You may not be able to pick up these unusual shaped pots easily and so may not be able to give the plants their ideal conditions, but you can use the common types of clay pots that are available in most towns. Once, however, you get really keen on the cultivation of succulents, you will find it worth ordering a certain number of the special pots required from a good pot maker.

1   Cacti and other succulents on a windowsill

2   *Cereus peruvianus monstruosus*

3   *Cephalocereus senilis*

6

Some easy-to-grow cacti and other succulents

Anybody who has visited the Cactus and Succulent House at one of the major botanical gardens in this country, will have been impressed not only by the great variation in the plants but also by the tremendous number of different kinds of plants that can be grown. Naturally, the average plant shop will only have a limited selection to offer and even the cactus specialist may not have unlimited stocks. It is well for the beginner to have some idea as to what plants he is most likely to be successful with right at the start. It is not encouraging to spend a lot of money on starting a collection, only to find that the majority of the plants need extra special treatment or hothouse conditions.

Without any doubt the best way to keep cacti and other succulents in the British climate is in a glasshouse, where it is much easier to obtain the correct conditions of temperature, light and humidity, etc., than in a sitting room or bedroom, for instance. There are, however, countless thousands of small collections in sunny windows throughout the country and an enormous number of people derive great enjoyment from them. The most important rule is to choose the sunniest window possible, and then to follow carefully the advice given with regard to the care of the plants.

Over-watering becomes doubly dangerous during the winter months, when the temperature of the living-room in which the plants are situated drops during the night or when the family is away for the week-end. We can also sincerely advise the beginner to start with plants that are easy to handle and leave such genera as *Echinocactus* and *Ferocactus*, which are noted for their spines, until later when more experience has been gained.

Every collector should try to obtain a plant of *Pereskia* of some sort; *P. grandifolia* and *P. aculeata rubescens* are to be recommended, the former for its flowers and the latter for its leaves. Both require a little more shade than other cacti and a slightly peatier soil.

5 *Lobivia famatimensis cristata*

4 *Astrophytum capricorne aureum*

7 *Ferocactus electracanthus*

6 *Gymnocalycium saglione*

No collection would be complete without some of the Prickly Pears, although the beginner with a small greenhouse or windowsill would be well advised to stick to some of the smaller growing varieties such as the *Opuntia microdasys* varieties. *Austrocylindropuntia salmiana* is also a good variety to grow since it flowers quite easily and is a good representative of the more treelike plants. *Brasilopuntia brasiliensis* remains short but it is more like the characteristic Prickly Pears, although a shy flowerer.

The upright columnar cacti are a prerequisite for any collection that aims to be representative. *Stetsonia coryne* has attractive black spines although it is fairly slow growing. *Oreocereus celsianus* has attractive woolly hairs almost completely covering its brown spines. *Cleistocactus straussii* is also a good ornament to any collection with its sleeky white hairs. *Trichocereus spachianus* is an extremely robust columnar cactus often used for grafting stock and *Trichocereus pasacana* is a lower, more barrel-shaped plant, with attractive spines. *Eulychnia floresii* is also attractive with white edges and black spines. *Carnegiea gigantea* is famous as the Saguaro, national flower of Arizona, and is easily obtained although very slow growing.

The Old Man Cactus, *Cephalocereus senilis*, is easy to get hold of and is always an object of interest; its hair is so long it can be combed, but it is also very slow growing. *Myrtillocactus geometrizans* is a good plant to have in any collection, it is quick growing and branches easily. *Lophocereus schottii* is often available in shops—do not be misled by its natural brownish tinge into thinking that it is dead. Of the true *Cereus*, *Cereus peruvianus* and *Cereus peruvianus monstruosus* are to be recommended; *Cereus peruvianus* can be easily flowered in its fifth or sixth year. *Espostoa lanata* is another of the Old Man Cacti but somewhat faster growing than *Cephalocereus senilis*.

Selenicereus boeckmannii and *Selenicereus grandiflorus* do very well when planted against a sunny wall in a greenhouse and are most attractive when they produce their huge showy white flowers at midnight. *Hylocereus undatus* is more vigorous and also flowers at night. The Rat's Tail Cactus, *Aporocactus flagelliformis*, is a very popular plant with its hanging green stems and abundantly produced red flowers, although care must be taken to prevent the stems rotting back and for this reason they are often grafted.

Echinopsis multiplex is probably one of the most easily obtained cacti and, although most specimens seldom flower, a really long winter rest, coupled with a complete absence of nitrate based fertilisers such as dried blood, can induce the most attractive flowers on this plant. *Echinopsis rhodotricha* is also a worthwhile addition to any collection although another shy flowerer.

One of the most beautiful members of this group of cacti is *Pseudolobivia kratochvilleana*. In the spring when it is in flower its small green body is

8 *Echinocereus fitchii*. For a really showy plant, this is hard to beat

9 *Aylostera pseudodeminuta*. Also known as *Rebutia pseudodeminuta*. Easy to grow and flowers very early

10 *Aylostera deminuta*. This is a 'must' for every collection

11 *Gymnocalycium quehlianum*. Its white flowers have a red throat

12 *Gymnocalycium venturianum*. Its deep red flowers make it an excellent addition to any collection

13 *Gymnocalycium damsii*. Produces large numbers of white flowers in succession from May to September

14 *Mammillaria aurihamata.*
Forms an attractive golden
clump with white flowers

15 *Mammillaria heyderi.*
One of the first varieties to
flower, and has attractive
spines

16 *Mammillaria hahniana.*
Old Lady Cactus. The pale
yellow colour deepens
with age

17 *Top left Mammillaria rhodantha var*. Flowers later in the year
18 *Top right Mammillaria uncinata*. This cactus is very tolerant

19 *Above Mammillaria zeilmanniana alba*. The white form of No. 20
20 *Left Mammillaria zeilmanniana*. Especially suitable for the beginner but care should be taken as it rots off easily

21 *Rebutia (Mediolobivia) pygmaea.* Flowers when quite tiny

22 *Notocactus tabularis.* A very tolerant plant which flowers when quite young

23 *Parodia sanguiniflora.* This makes a showy addition to any collection

24 *Parodia gracilis*. Every collector should try to obtain this plant. It flowers almost continuously throughout the summer

25 *Parodia microsperma*. Flowers are of a wide range of colours, from red to yellow

26 *Parodia chrysacanthion*. Produces flowers very freely early in the year

27 *Setiechinopsis mirabilis*.
Night flowering, slightly
scented

28 *Pseudolobivia kratochvilleana*. The enormous white,
slightly scented flowers
completely dwarf its body

9 *Rhipsalidopsis rosea*. This
will grow in a shady position

30 Hybrid between *Schlum-bergera gaertneri* and *Rhip-salidopsis rosea*, recently in-troduced

31 *Rebutia* hybrid. A typi-cal 'flower of the desert'

32 *Rebutia* hybrid. Every collection should include this easily flowered hybrid

completely dwarfed by enormous white, slightly scented flowers which are borne on the end of six inch tubes from the side of the plant. The Peanut Cactus, *Chamaecereus silvestrii* is a good grower and has attractive orange flowers; although the young joints break off easily they can be equally easily rooted. There is also a yellow form which is becoming more generally available called *Chamascereus silvestrii luteus*, but this *must* be grafted.

Every collection should include a representative of the genus *Lobivia*, named after the country in which it occurs—Bolivia. We recommend *Lobivia famatimensis* (often sold as *L. densispina*) which is easy to flower and can be obtained in a wide variety of colours, and also *Lobivia aurea* (syn. *Pseudolobivia aurea*) whose yellow flowers are borne on robust tubes.

Mediolobivia pygmaea can at first easily be mistaken for a *Rebutia*, and was formerly known as *Rebutia haagei*; it flowers when quite tiny.

Aylostera deminuta is a 'must' for every collection and upwards of thirty flowers can be induced on quite young plants of only three years of age. The Rebutias are similar and should also be represented in any collection, especially since they are the easiest of all cacti to flower. To be recommended are *Rebutia minuscula*, with red flowers, *Rebutia marsoneri*, with yellow flowers, and *Rebutia violaciflora*, with lilac-coloured flowers. *Rebutia senilis*, which should produce red flowers if it is the true species, is characterised by soft white spines.

For a really showy plant it is hard to beat *Echinocereus fitchii* which makes fluorescent pink flowers. *Echinocereus stramineus* has attractive straw-like spines but is not so easy to flower.

The next family of cacti, the Echinocactanae, is characterised by the way the flower buds unfold with the spines from the growing point at the top of the plant. *Matucana aurantiaca* (claimed by some botanists to be of the family Cereeae) is one of this group which every beginner should try and obtain since its showy orange flowers of a somewhat curious tubular shape are produced towards the end of the season when there is little else in flower.

Acanthocalycium violaceum produces magenta-coloured flowers when it is about four years old, amidst brown papery spines.

As long as they are not over-potted, Parodias will grow and flower well in a small collection. However, when in pots they make few roots and it is therefore important that they have a well-drained compost. We recommend *Parodia aureispina* and the somewhat similar *Parodia aurihamata*, both of which have golden spines, although the former has a more orange coloured flower, while the latter is more yellow. *Parodia chrysacanthion*, which has long golden spines, also produces flowers very freely and is the first of this family to produce flowers during the year. *Parodia sanguiniflora* makes a showy addition to any collection with its bright red flowers, and even showier although slightly less free with them is *Parodia rubriflora*.

Parodia rubellihamata is a very attractively shaped plant with a whorl of small spines and a magnificent cluster of yellow flowers. *Parodia microsperma* produces variously coloured flowers and has long hooked spines. *Parodia mutabilis* with yellow flowers is also a worthwhile variety. And every collector should try and obtain a plant of *Parodia gracilis* whose small orange flowers fight their way up through the brown spines at the top of the plant almost right through the summer.

By following these outlines and obtaining the above mentioned species, it is possible for someone with only a limited amount of space to have a Parodia in flower almost the whole summer through.

Wigginsia erinaceus (formerly *Malacocarpus erinaceus*) is another favourite. It flowers when still quite small at about four years old.

The *Notocactus* most commonly found in all collections is *Notocactus leninghaussii* which is popular on account of its sleek golden hairs. However, it is comparatively slow growing and it is most unusual for plants to flower until they are nine inches high. Some other *Notocacti* flower much more easily and are also readily obtained. *Notocactus ottonis* is a robust plant to start with and those who have only a limited amount of space would do well to get plants of *Notocactus tabularis*, *Notocactus concinnus*, *Notocactus muricatus*, and *Notocactus apricus*.

These are all very similar, very tough and flower when quite small, normally producing their first flowers when about two years old. The flowers of all *Notocacti* in this group are yellow in colour and open fully at mid-day. *Notocactus submammulosus* produces a far less ragged flower than the others since the petals are more rounded at the ends; its near relative *N. submammulosus* var. *pampeanus* is characterised by fewer larger spines and more pointed petals.

Notocactus scopa should be a welcome addition to any collection since it has an attractive covering of white spines tipped with red all the year round and freely produces yellow flowers in the summer. They are, however, slightly smaller than in all the previous species. Amongst the newer introductions in this family, we recommend *Notocactus horstii*, sometimes sold as *Notocactus juncineus*. This has orange flowers and appears at first to be similar to a *Parodia*. It is a good plant for the small collection since it flowers nearer the end of the season when everything else is finished.

The next group of cacti are the 'Chin Cacti' so called from the bulging areoles. Botanically they are distinguished by the absence of spines on the calyx. Good ones to start with are *Gymnocalycium damsii* which produces large numbers of whitish flowers in succession from May to September, *Gymnocalycium quehlianum*, which is larger and whose flowers have a red throat, and

Gymnocalycium mihanovichii which has a slightly variegated body with yellowish green flowers and is also available as a 'Hibotan' variety.

This last group have plant bodies in various colours such as red, yellow, pink and white. However, they are somewhat delicate, seldom produce a true flower and always have to be grafted. *Gymnocalycium bruchii* is another worthwhile variety which stays small and compact, forming dense clumps.

The Golden Barrel, or Grandmother's Armchair, otherwise known as *Echinocactus grusonii* is often seen in cultivation in small collections; care should be taken not to give it too strong sunlight as it seems to burn very easily.

Astrophytums, the Bishop's Cap Cacti, are now becoming more and more popular. *Astrophytum ornatum* and the hybrids normally available have attractively flecked bodies and shapely spines. *Astrophytum myriostigma* has a more intense flecking on it and flowers quite easily. Among many collectors the four sided plants of the latter are greatly prized.

Ferocacti are vicious plants and are only really attractive while the spines are young and intensely coloured. The ones most often available are *Ferocactus wislizenii* and *Ferocactus electracanthus*.

One of the standbys of any collection should always be *Hamatocactus setispinus*. This starts producing its yellow flowers with red centres in May and goes on until the plants are put to rest in the autumn, when one may still enjoy the brilliant red berries which follow if the flowers have been correctly pollinated.

The *Echinofossulocacti* are remarkable for their deeply divided ribs which are deeply wrinkled. The easiest to flower is *E. zacatecasensis*. *Thelocactus bicolor* is often known as the Rainbow Cactus because of the peculiar variety of colours visible in the spines when they are wet.

Next among the true cacti we come to the Mammillarias. They are probably the biggest single genus of cacti and of the enormous variety available we recommend the following as being especially suitable for the beginner. *Mammillaria zeilmanniana* has red flowers and is also obtainable in a white form as *M. zeilmanniana alba*. *Mammillaria schelhasei* produces curious greenish yellow flowers in great profusion.

Mammillaria heyderi is one of the first varieties to flower and also has most attractive spines. *Mammillaria heeriana* forms fine upright plants and produces rings of red tubular flowers. *Mammillaria wildii* and *Mammillaria woodsii* are both tough, quick growing varieties. *Mammillaria centricirrha* needs to be quite old before it will flower but is attractive even when not in flower, so too is *Mammillaria kewensis*, another plant which flowers towards the end of the summer. One of the more unusual Mammillarias is *Mammillaria camptotricha* which has curious straw-like spines on the end of long tubercles.

Dolicothele longimamma, which is sometimes sold as a Mammillaria, is a most ornamental plant and produces large yellow flowers extending well beyond the spines.

Lastly in this review of the cactus family we come to what are commonly called the Leaf Cacti; the ones most commonly seen in the shops include *Schlumbergera gaertneri*, the Whitsun Cactus, *Zygocactus truncatus*, the Christmas Cactus, and the recently introduced hybrids between *Schlumbergera gaertneri* and *Rhipsalidopsis rosea* which are available in pink, violet and carmine.

These will be more clearly differentiated from one another in a later part of this book, but provided there is an abundance of hanging space they are attractive assets to any collection.

Of the Epiphyllums or Leaf Cacti the only one which we can warmly recommend to the beginner are *Epiphyllum* 'Elegantissimum' which makes quite large flowers even when the plant is quite small and *Nopalxochia phyllanthoides* var. 'Deutsche Kaiserin' which has attractive pink flowers and stays relatively compact.

Other succulents

There are some species of Adromiscus which, although slow growing, are not difficult to cultivate and are most interesting on account of their curious habit of growth. *Adromischus maculatus* and *Adromischus cooperi* are worth trying.

Most Aeoniums are easy to grow but they tend to lose their original graceful habit with age. *Aeonium simsii* is one which stays short and *Aeonium arboreum atropurpureum*, which has attractive dark purple leaves, maintains its graceful shape.

Nearly everyone has at some time possessed a specimen of the Partridge Breasted Aloe, *Aloe variegata*, which appreciates more shade than most succulents, and another favourite is *Aloe aristata* which has rather thin leaves arranged to form a dense rosette. *Aloe ferox* and *Aloe arborescens* are also good plants with which the beginner can start.

Anacampseros rufescens is a very interesting, although slow growing, plant. Its pale pink flowers need extremely strong sunlight to open and it is quite an idea to put them under a 250w. photographic lamp once the buds are formed.

Argyroderma arctophyllum and *A. testiculare* are fairly easy to obtain and can be cultivated without much trouble. *Bergeranthus multiceps* is one of the Mesembryanthemum family that can go in a small collection.

The Ceropegias, near relations of the Stapelias, make good plants for the new enthusiast and if space allows the hanging *Ceropegia woodii* should be included in a collection.

There are over two hundred species of Conophytum and quite a number are easy to grow and usually obtainable. Try *Conophytum minutum* and *C. velutinum* for a start.

Many Crassulas make excellent plants to incorporate in a collection. *Crassula arborescens* is a fine dwarf shrub that makes an attractive 'tree' in a pot. *Crassula falcata* has grey leaves and a huge cluster of red flowers. *Crassula lycopodoides* is a strange moss-like plant which produces minute yellow flowers in the axils of its dense leaves. Various forms of this species are also occasionally available. *Crassula perforata* is a fine variety with perfoliate leaves, but should be cut back occasionally to prevent it becoming too leggy.

Another good variety is *Crassula schmidtii*, which forms a low growing clump with spotted leaves. It does best when propagated afresh each year from cuttings, as once a rosette has produced the little pink flowers, fresh shoots grow from the side and it becomes leggy. *Crassula socialis* is a pretty plant which can be grown in a shallow pan and allowed to spread.

Cotyledon undulata is another plant often seen in collections on account of its beautiful wavy-edged grey leaves and its attractive flowers which are produced on comparatively long stems.

'Wandering Sailor' is one of the most popular and the easiest of house plants to grow and the collector of succulents should try to obtain a plant of its succulent relative, *Cyanotis somaliensis*. This plant grows well, but it is a good idea to cut back the shoots as they develop and to root the tips in order to keep the plant more compact.

Echeverias are native to Central and South America and fall into two main groups: those that have short or non-existent stems and those which form large stems and turn eventually into a small shrub. Among the former is the popular *Echeveria derenbergii*. *Echeveria gibbiflora* and its variety *metallica* are both assets to a collection but may require staking. The former can readily be had in flower at Christmas and makes for interest at a time when there are few other flowers.

One of the more curious plants which a beginner should try to obtain as it will lend great interest to any collection is *Echidnopsis cereiformis* with its strange, undivided flowers.

The Euphorbias are one of the largest families of succulents and have a great variety of different forms. *Euphorbia trigona* (often sold as 'Hermentiana') is a good indoor one needing slightly more shade and warmth in winter than cacti. *Euphorbia caput-medusae* and its cristate form are both becoming more frequent in the shops and are rewarding on account of their rapid growth. *Euphorbia submammillaris* is also to be recommended for the collector with limited space. *Euphorbia meloformis*, *Euphorbia obesa* and *Euphorbia valida*, although not so fast growing, are nevertheless interesting for their unusual appearance and are extremely tough.

The Crown of Thorns is another variety of Euphorbia which is easily obtained; this is normally *Euphorbia millii*, *Euphorbia millii* var. *splendens*, or the yellow variety which has just become available *Euphorbia millii* Tanarive; all appreciate slightly more warmth in the winter and a little shade in summer. Do not be alarmed if these three drop their leaves on being brought into the home as they will make good their losses in no time at all, and they always tend to lose a few leaves when moved.

Faucaria tigrina is an attractive little plant with jaw-like leaves and pretty yellow flowers, but it is extremely susceptible to mealy bug and should be examined regularly for this pest.

Haworthias are good plants for the beginner to try since they can easily be induced to flower on a windowsill and stay relatively compact. *Haworthia cuspidata* and *Haworthia papillosa* are both good varieties in this respect.

Hoyas are also steadily growing in popularity and two varieties generally available are *Hoya carnosa* and *Hoya carnosa variegata*. Although the plain green form can be flowered without too much difficulty, the variegated form flowers very seldom.

Kalanchoes exhibit a wide variety of habit ranging from the Tom Thumb varieties which are cultivated for their gaily coloured flowers to the much larger varieties such as *Kalanchoes beharensis* which are covered with dense hairs. The genus includes species such as the Mother of Thousands, *Kalanchoe daigremontiana*, which produces live plantlets round the edges of the leaves, and *Kalanchoe tubiflora* which is similar. Other varieties commonly seen are *Kalanchoe fedtschenkoi* fa. *marginata* with grey-red and cream variegated leaves and *Kalanchoe blossfeldiana* hybrids with dark green leaves and a dense head of yellow or red flowers.

Lampranthus aurantiacus is a member of the Mesembryanthemum family and is widely cultivated as a bedding plant. If grown in a greenhouse it must be kept under-potted and under control as it spreads fast; it requires full sunlight to produce any flowers.

Lithops exercise a strange fascination for collectors on account of the extraordinary way in which they mimic the surrounding soil. *Lithops* do best when planted in a pot with a narrow top and a lot of depth, rather more conical than the average pot that one sees on the market; the beginner should try the larger ones first and in winter take extra precautions against mice as they will attack *Lithops* and similar plants before any others in their search for food.

Echeveria harmsii is a plant with red and yellow flowers, widely cultivated as a small shrub; it is sometimes sold as *Oliveranthus elegans*.

Orostachys spinosus, although perfectly hardy, is sometimes sold in a pot and may be cultivated in the greenhouse. In appearance it is similar to a *Sempervivum* to which it is closely related.

Similar to the *Lithops* is *Pleiospilos bolusii*; the family name is derived from two Greek words meaning 'full of spots'. The leaves are shaped exactly like two angular chips of rock and cunningly hidden; it can be more difficult to detect than a Lithops. The yellow flowers can be up to 3 in. in diameter.

Rhombophyllum rhomboideum and *Rhombophyllum nellii* are both good varieties for the beginner. They are similar appearance to *Pleiospilos* but without spots.

Mother-in-Law's Tongue, *Sanseveria trifasciata* 'Laurentii', is probably one of the most commonly seen succulents and certainly one of the most indestructible. We have heard of some plants which have lived for years on a teaspoonful of water each day.

The hardy varieties of Sedums are outside the scope of this book. For the collector with a greenhouse they make an attractive foil to his collection when planted outside. Three of the tender varieties are to be recommended for the beginner—*Sedum pachyphyllum* whose grey, very succulent leaves are arranged densely round the stem, *Sedum lineare variegatum* which has small pointed variegated leaves and *Sedum sieboldii medio-variegatum*, the leaves of which have a white patch in the centre and are followed by heads of pink flowers in late summer.

Sempervivums are all hardy plants commonly known as Houseleeks. A good collection can best be obtained from suppliers of rockery plants and they are best grown outside since they tend to become very leggy and lose their characteristics when grown in a greenhouse.

Curiously enough, the common Ragwort of Britain has succulent relatives. The similarity is only apparent in the flowers which clearly resemble one another but the habit can be completely different as in *Senecio articulatus* var. *globosus* which has almost spherical stem segments and *Senecio macroglossus variegatus* which closely resembles an Ivy.

Stapelias are an unusual asset to any collection and should be included. However, the species is pollinated by blow flies and in order to attract them the flowers give off a smell like rotting meat, so if you are sensitive to smells it is best to avoid them; alternatively they may be placed outside while in flower. The most commonly cultivated species is *Stapelia variegata* which produces yellow flowers with brick coloured flecks in them.

Tradescantia navicularis is a very close relative of the Wandering Sailor but has succulent boat-shaped leaves which give it its name.

No list would be complete without mentioning Yuccas. These are Agave-shaped plants which will produce a magnificent spike of flowers in their fifth year; however, only the owner of a large greenhouse should attempt to grow them indoors as they grow to a considerable size. *Yucca filamentosa* and *Yucca gloriosa* are both hardy in all but the coldest climates.

7

Planting and transplanting

There is one thing about cacti and other succulents which beginners especially will appreciate: the plants, because they grow slowly, need transplanting very infrequently. If one needs a simple rule, it is that transplanting may take place annually, in the case of plants which have become as large as one's fist. When they have grown larger than this and are, therefore, by inference in bigger pots, they do not require transplanting more than once every three or four years. The really big heavy specimens that grow in parks and in botanical gardens are not transplanted at all, but some of the soil may be taken away and some fresh compost added in its place every five years or so. When this kind of work is done the greatest of care must be taken to prevent any injury to the roots.

As to the young seedlings, it is interesting to note that it is quite good to leave them in their boxes or pans for, say, two years. For some reason or another they seem to like one another's company! After two years they can be potted up separately, but even then the pots may be stood quite close together on the staging of the greenhouse. As a general rule, one can say that for young plants a change of soil is advisable every two years.

One must bear in mind that the important thing is to keep the plant going well especially in the first seven years of its life. This means that there must always be room in the pot for the roots and that there must always be some nutriment for these roots to pass up to the plant itself.

Time to transplant
The best time to transplant is undoubtedly the spring, when the plant is starting into growth again. In Britain, most of the work will be done during the month of March. It pays to have clean pots and crocks, and to sterilise them they can always be stood in boiling water for ten minutes or so if made of

clay. If old pots are used, it is a good thing to scrub them well first, while if the pots are new, they should be stood in cold water for two days before the sterilisation takes place. Some gardeners add a teaspoonful of permanganate of potash crystals to each 2 gallons of boiling water used. Plastic pots can be cleaned with a medium formaldehyde solution such as is used for de-scaling kettles.

Having made certain that the pots and crocks are clean, the compost should be made up carefully as advised in chapter 3. It should stand for some time in the greenhouse so that it warms up, or if this is impossible, a brick may be put into a hot oven for two hours and then this is stood on the potting shed bench and the soil mixture to be used is then put over the top in a mound so that it is warmed.

Method of transplanting

Take the plant that is to be re-potted, invert it and then, wearing a thick glove, hold the plant firmly in one hand and tap one edge of the pot on the bench. A sharp tap is all that is necessary. It will be found that the plant will come out of its pot perfectly in such a manner that the roots are quite un-damaged and the ball of soil remains whole. Remove the crocks at the base of the plant, tease out the roots a little at the base and, at the same time, look out for insect pests on the roots, especially mealy bugs. If these are present, the roots should be dipped in a weak solution of Malathion. This can be made up by dissolving one fluid ounce of Malathion in 3 gallons (13·6 lit.) of water. When using Malathion always wear gloves and follow the manufacturer's instructions.

With a pair of tweezers, or some similar instrument, start to remove the old compost. Do this carefully so as not to damage the roots. If, however, you come across a group of roots which are matted together and dead, these may be cut out altogether. If any roots are broken during the operation, cut them with an old razor blade so that the wound is clean and clear. After any damage of this kind it is quite a good thing to give a light dusting to the cut roots with a powder hormone, which can be obtained from any good horticultural chemist.

Once the majority of old soil has been removed (don't overdo this and thus damage the roots), start to pot on, as it is called. Use a pot a little larger than the original one, from a 3 in. (7·6 cm) pot, for instance, you can pot on to a 4½ in. (11·3 cm), or from a 4½ in. (11·3 cm) to a 6 in. (15·2 cm) pot. Incidentally, if you are mystified by the terms used in the trade for the sizes of pots, it will be as well to know that the 3 in. (7·6 cm) pots are 60s, the 4½ in. (11·3 cm) pots 54s and the 5½ in. (14 cm) pots 48s. The numbers refer to the pots that can be cast from a definite sized lump of clay.

Put plenty of crocks into the bottom of the new pot, i.e. to a depth of say 1 inch. The bottom crock of all had better be concave and rest happily over the drainage hole. On top of the crocks, place a handful of sedge peat, which will act as a kind of barrier/sieve between the perfect drainage below and the compost above. Hold the plant in position in the middle of the pot, so that the roots are properly spread out. Scoop out the compost with the other hand and pour it in gradually all round the plant, turning the pot from time to time so as to make certain that an even amount of compost is deposited all round. Every now and then tap the pot lightly on the bench, so as to cause the compost to settle.

Don't try and make the compost too firm; it will settle down sufficiently hard later on. Leave about half an inch (1·3 cm) at the top for watering. See that the cactus or succulent is planted at the exact depth it was before. Put in the label immediately, before it is forgotten. The potting soil should be just moist and this means that when the potting on has been completed no further water should be given for fourteen days. The idea is to encourage new root hairs to develop in the warm, sufficiently moist compost, and if water is given it will cool down the soil as well as filling up some of the air spaces.

In the case of a somewhat large *Mammillaria*, there is always the danger of thinking that the lower portion of the stem is really a tuberous root. Some amateurs in this belief have potted on plants too deeply. The great thing is to look for the previous soil mark and if anything to plant a little more shallowly than more deeply. If it is possible, the newly potted on specimens should go somewhere where they will get a little more warmth than before, especially bottom heat. For this reason gardeners often put them on a box 'sitting' just above the hot water pipes. Here they will not only get bottom heat but also a little extra shade, which they will appreciate as they are getting acclimatised to their new compost and container.

8

Seed sowing

People often have different points of view over the question of seed sowing in the case of cacti. Some affirm that it is not really worth while because most seedlings grow slowly. The gardener, therefore, has to wait a number of years before he has plants which really make a show. Furthermore, of course, beginners don't want large numbers of plants of the same species or variety. They prefer to buy little plants from nurserymen who specialise in this work.

Some species such as Rebutias and Fraileas can be flowered in 2 years from seed sowing and the raising of plants from seed is not too difficult for the amateur.

Every year in fact hundreds of plants are raised in this way in many parts of the country. Nurserymen on the whole concentrate their attention on sowing the seeds of the quick growing types and they propagate the slow growing species vegetatively or by grafting.

Time of sowing

Seeds may be sown under glass any time from, say, the middle of April to the middle of October. Most experts, however, advise not to attempt sowing seed until the temperature outside is normally about 17°C (65°F) in the shade. The temperature of the greenhouse should be about 22°C (70°F) and the compost used should be the one described in chapter 3. It is claimed that the seeds keep best when they are kept in their berries. It is, however, better on the whole to sow the seeds immediately after they have been harvested rather than to wait several months or even a year.

Most seeds germinate quite quickly, but there are species of Opuntias which may prove rather slow. Put plenty of broken crooks in the bottom of a shallow pot or pan and fill this to within one-third of its depth. Prepare the compost and place this on top, pressing it down very lightly. Make certain that it is quite level and see that it is within a quarter of an inch of the top of the container. Now mix the seeds well with enough sand to cover the top of the tray, sprinkle this mixture on top of the seed compost so that it forms a fine even layer. In the majority of cases no further covering is necessary. Sow the seeds evenly aiming to space them about 1 inch apart. The only seeds needing covering are the larger ones, e.g. Astrophytums, and they should be levelled up with sand to one-eight of an inch (3 mm). Press them down lightly after sowing into the soil with a flat piece of wood.

Now take the pan or pot and immerse it carefully and gently in a basin of rain water so that the soaking will be done from below. Never allow any of the water to get over the sides. It is most important not to disturb the thin layer of silver sand on the top. Place the pan on the staging of the greenhouse at a temperature of 22°C (70°F), covered with a sheet of glass and newspaper. Germination should take place at the end of a week, but don't be surprised if some of the seedlings do not appear for three or four weeks.

In some years and in some districts a kind of green growth appears on the surface of the soil and this may impede the proper germination of the seeds. This Algal growth, as it is called, can usually be prevented if the box is watered with a solution of Copper Sulphate four days before the seeds are sown. To make up the solution you need one teaspoonful of Copper Sulphate crystals to one quart of water. Incidentally, it is curious the way seedlings do not germinate well when they are exposed to bright light. Some gardeners, for this reason, have used a glass sheet over a box painted over with a green solution known as Summer Cloud. This sheet of glass has to be lifted off and wiped every day to remove the moisture which forms on the lower side.

The moment the seedlings appear, the glass should be raised somewhat and the tilt should always be away from the sun so that the plants continue to get the necessary shade. Gradually, of course, the glass is raised higher and higher until it is removed altogether.

For those who are raising plants from seed for the first time, there is something to be said for starting with some of the Cereus group, say *Cereus peruvianus*. The reason is that the seeds are larger on the whole and so they are easier to sow and in addition the seedlings grow very quickly and thus results are seen quickly—always an encouragement I think! Many of the seeds of the Parodias are very tiny indeed and take a good deal of handling and thought it can be said Opuntias grow quickly once they have germinated, they certainly are slow to make a start and this, for a beginner, is discouraging.

It is also very discouraging to find that a number of the little seedlings have damped off when they have just started to grow well. Do, therefore, take the necessary precautions to prevent this either by watering the box with the solution advised on page 17, or you can use Cheshunt Compound, obtainable from any good chemist. It is better to lower the box carefully into a bowl containing this solution so as to let it soak up naturally.

Suggested compost

A good compost in which to sow the seeds consists of 2 parts sterilised loam, 1 part fine sedge peat, 1 part coarse sharp silver sand and 1 part finely crushed brick, adding to this mixture 2 tablespoonfuls of carbonate of lime for each 2-gallon bucket made up. Those who want to sterilise a small quantity of soil can put it into a biscuit tin and place this in a really hot oven. A potato the size of a hen's egg may be buried in the centre an inch down and when it is cooked the soil will be ready to use.

Filling the box

See that the base of the box has the necessary drainage holes at the four corners and in the centre. These can be made with a brace and bit or even a red hot poker. Dip the box in Rentokil so as to preserve it. Put in plenty of broken crocks or broken brick bats so that about half the box is filled up with this rough material. Lay on top of these broken crocks sedge peat to the depth of a quarter of an inch and then put the compost over the top; level it and press it down fairly firm. There should be no need to dip it in the chemical solution mentioned on page 51 if the soil is sterilised and if sedge peat is used.

Sowing the seeds

Those who start with large seeds, as advised, should aim to space them out half an inch apart. There is not much difficulty in doing this if you take up one seed at a time on the end of a knife blade or spatula and thus actually place the seed in its right position. If the seeds are too small to do this, the best thing is to mix them with sand as described above on page 50.

It is possible, of course, to sow three or four species in one box and all one has to do is to divide up the area with small strips of bamboo laid flat on the soil. Thus it is possible to have several little compartments, each one sown with a different type of cactus. It is important to label the compartments immediately and the modern aluminium strips are ideal for this purpose. They can be inscribed with a pencil and they last almost for ever.

The larger seeds can just be pressed into the compost. The smaller ones are better left on the surface of the compost.

Watering

The compost used must always be just moist. It must never be sodden and never be dry. It is, therefore, convenient to dip the box in tepid water down to half its depth. This must be done very slowly and after the dipping, the box must be stood aside for a moment so as to allow the excess moisture to drain away, before it is put back onto the shelving of the house. This dipping will normally be carried out every three days. During the whole of this period, the box should be kept at a temperature of 22°C (70°F). That is why it is important to use water at a similar temperature. Many species will germinate quite well at 17°C (65°F). The gardener must decide the economic temperature which will suit his purpose and keep that temperature constant. It is most important not to allow great 'ups' and 'downs'.

Signs of failure
If the little seedlings appear to be rotting off at the base, then the trouble is invariably damping-off which has been encouraged by over-watering.

If the seedlings adopt a reddy-brown colour, this is a sign that the compost has been kept too dry and that watering has not been done regularly enough.

If the seedlings appear to stand still and not to progress at all and they have a brownish shade to them, then it is invariably an indication that they are in too strong sunshine, and they must be shaded.

Bottom heat
In order that the box or pan may have the necessary shade coupled with bottom heat, it is quite a good idea to make up a wooden tray, say 3 ft (91 cm) long and about 18 in. (45·7 cm) wide. Put some damp sedge peat in the bottom and place the boxes or pans of seedlings in this. Then place this tray just above the hot water pipes in a shady part of the greenhouse and germination should be good. Furthermore, the seedlings should grow hard and compact with the result that they will be able to be transplanted without any difficulty.

Some people like to try and do the sowing in the sunless seasons of the year and so they raise most of their plants during the months of January and February. If the method in the previous paragraph is adopted, it is wise to lift the tray from just above the hot water pipes and place this on the staging of the greenhouse once all the seedlings are through.

It is possible to provide bottom heat electrically and those who are interested should consult their local electricity board who have leaflets available on the subject.

Transplanting the seedlings
The seedlings should be transplanted as soon as they become so crowded in their container that they are touching one another. The transplanting should

normally be into another tray, unless the plants are very big. Care should be taken when moving the seedlings not to damage the minute root systems or to crush the small plant bodies. Make a little wooden fork and, at the same time, sharpen a piece of wood so that it comes to a point similar to that of a small pencil.

Now lift the baby seedling out by pushing the fork into the compost just below and levering up slightly. Then use the pointed stick so as to leave the cactus seedling sitting in the wedge of the fork. Have a box of baby-pots near by and with the pointed stick make a hole where the baby cactus has to grow for the next few months.

See that the roots of the seedlings go straight down into the hole and, using the pointed stick once more, press the compost lightly around these roots. Remove the fork by slipping it away gradually and use the pointed stick to scratch around the plant, so as to leave the compost level. When boxes are used, the next seedling should be half an inch (1·3 cm) away and in fact they all should be planted on the half an inch basis.

Where it is possible (and it is with an electrically heated or gas heated greenhouse) increase the heat by about 5 or 6°F (3°C) the first week after transplanting and that will give the plants a boost because it encourages root development. Try to give a second transplanting, this time to an inch apart in the boxes some 3–4 weeks later. It is not advisable, however, to transplant after the middle of October and any movement of seedlings is better delayed after that date until the spring.

When little pots are used (these are the ones usually bought as 2-in. (5 cm) pots) a quarter of a pot should be filled with broken pots or little stones and the rest with the compost advised for the boxes. The plan is to put sufficient over the drainage material for the base of the ball of roots to rest on when the bottom of the seed leaves (the globular cacti of course have no seed leaves) is level with the top of the pot. With a teaspoon take some more of the dry compost and pour it around the base of the plant so as to fill the pot up to the top and then tap the pot gently on the bench to firm the soil; this should settle the soil around the roots. If, when this is done, there seems insufficient compost present a little more may be added. A second tapping should be given and all will be well.

Place the little pots on a sieve or riddle and then when they are all together, dip them in the water as advised for the boxes. They will need dipping in this way every week or so if the weather is sunny. It is surprising how long the plants can be allowed to grow in these tiny pots. They will certainly be there for a year, and maybe more. The great mistake beginners make is to go on re-potting and potting on every six months: the results are always disastrous.

The authors have had various types of cacti in the same pot for four years and more without any disturbance at all. Many of the specimens were quite strong growing, but they didn't seem to resent the constriction of the roots. This is, of course, the exception rather than the rule, but it does show what these fascinating plants will put up with.

Gardeners who like to sow the seeds in April should do the first transplanting in June and the second about mid-September. This means that the plants are growing well in their new pots or boxes before the winter sets in, and they are perfectly happy 'dozing' from early November until late February. It is during that period that they want a minimum of water.

If, for some reason or another, it is necessary to sow the seed in the autumn, then no transplanting at all is done until the spring. Sometimes thirty or forty per cent. of the seed will germinate before the winter sets in and the rest will remain dormant until the spring. Those, however, that do remain dormant, may easily catch the others up because they will grow so quickly when once they start.

If, by any chance, a mistake is made when a seedling is got out of a pan and all the roots are torn off, one need not despair, for, providing the baby plant is nice and plump and sound, the seedling can be planted very shallowly in some quite dry compost and in the course of a few weeks or so it will send out another series of roots quite happily.

9

How to take cuttings and graft

Cuttings

It is really surprising how easily most cacti can be propagated by cuttings. The secret is to start with a mixture of sedge peat and coarse silver sand in equal parts. The peat should be just on the damp side. When the cutting has been severed from the parent plant, it should be laid aside for two or three days so that the base can dry out. After this, it can be pushed into the peat and sand so that the base is buried about half an inch. Now the scheme is to keep the box or pot in which the cutting or cuttings have been placed at a temperature of 22°C (70°F).

The atmosphere should be 'close' also. This can be achieved in a greenhouse by covering the box, pot or pots with a four-sided cloche, or to have a little propagating frame on the bench of the greenhouse in which the box or pots may be placed.

It is possible to root small cuttings a day after they have been severed from the parent plant, but it is important to see that the base of the cutting is beautifully clean so the work must be done with the sharp blade of a knife or a razor blade. Some people have struck quite large cuttings which tend, for this reason, to be top-heavy. In this case it is necessary to push a length of bamboo into the peat and sand compost close to the cutting so that it may be tied up to it.

The peat used should be damp and then there will be no need to give any water for 10 days. In fact, the general rule is not to water any cuttings that have been taken until they have started to root. It is possible to take cuttings almost any time of the year, but the authors have found that it is easier to get the best results when the work is done say from 15th May to about the 20th August.

Some cacti, such as the *Opuntia spinosissima*, grow in a kind of jointed fashion. That is, a little prickly succulent leaf grows out of a much bigger lobe-

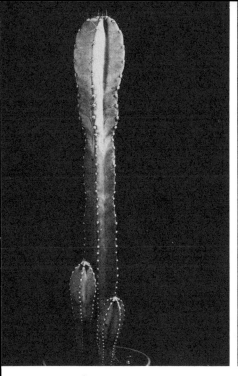

33 *Cereus peruvianus*

34 *Opuntia (Brasilopuntia) brasiliensis*

35 *Opuntia leucotricha*

36 *Opuntia* sp.

like leaf often called a 'pad'. These are not difficult to sever and they will strike as cuttings quite easily. Other cacti produce what may be called offshoots from the bottom of the plant. Regular clusters appear. In this case there is little difficulty in removing some of the offshoots, as one can, for instance, with *Mammillaria bocasana*, and these, of course, will strike extremely easily because they have almost started to make their own roots while attached to their parent plant.

Propagation of other succulents

It is true to say that it is possible to propagate most other succulents vege-tatively. The fleshy shoots strike comparatively easily; as in the case of cacti, it is important to make the cuts with the sharp blade of a knife and it is for this reason the authors recommend using a razor blade or one of those 'cut throat' razors still used by some barbers.

Once the cut has been made, the severed cuttings should be laid in a semi-shady spot, which must be nice and airy so as to allow the surface of the cut to heal over gradually. Some people dust the surface of the cut with powdered charcoal, but this is not really necessary.

The cuttings that strike easiest are those which are fairly well ripened, or should we say just a little woody. It is better not to take the really soft succulent side-shoots, because when these are inserted in sand they may rot off at the base. Succulent plants which produce a lot of milky fluid when cut should be treated with care. One should allow the excess sap to ooze out and no attempt should be made to insert the cutting in the sand or compost until the bleeding is complete. Some growers encourage this bleeding by immersing the base of the cuttings in water for half an hour or so.

Cuttings can be divided into two big classes: those which produce hardly any sap and which, therefore, dry in the matter of an hour or two and those which seem to ooze out a watery fluid for quite a long time and so, take longer to produce a little skin over the wound. One can take cuttings from the side shoots of a plant as well as cuttings from the terminal or end growth. The latter produce the most characteristic plants in the minimum of time. Side shoot cuttings take longer because they have, in the first place, to build up their new terminal shoot before they can be classed as typical of their 'kind'.

When to take cuttings

There are two good periods for taking cuttings: the first in the late summer, when growth is slowing up, and the second early in the spring before serious growth begins. It is a good thing to experiment. For instance, we have noticed that most of the Mesembryanthemums strike better when they are propagated late in the summer than in the spring.

The propagating frame
Though it is called a frame, it can be just a bottomless box covered with a sheet of glass. This may be stood on the staging of a greenhouse, preferably at a spot which is over the heating pipes, whether these are hot-water or electrical. The box should be filled with a compost consisting of 2 parts of sharp silver sand (which must not be sea-shore sand) and 1 part of fine sedge peat (not sphagnum peat). Fill the box to within 2 in. (5 cm) of the top with this compost, which should be just damp and which must be pressed down lightly with a wooden presser to make it quite level. Be sure that the corners of the boxes are just as firm as the centre.

It is a simple matter to push the individual cutting into the compost so that it is held up and is quite steady. Most cuttings will be put in perpendicularly, but leaf cuttings will be pushed in at an angle of 45° with the upper surface uppermost. Each cutting should have about an inch of room in which it can develop.

Once the cuttings are in position, the sheet of glass should be put on top and should not be removed at all except once a day about 9 a.m., when it should be lifted up in order that the moisture that will have collected on the underside, can be wiped off. Always expect the leaf-cuttings to take much longer to root than the stem, or shoot cuttings. The moment cuttings have rooted, they may be potted up individually as advised for cacti on page

Leaf cuttings
There are a number of succulents which can easily be propagated by means of their leaves. In fact some species of *Sedum*, which drop their leaves naturally in the summer, will often start to produce new plants of their own accord; for where the individual leaf touches the soil, it starts to grow. Some gardeners therefore lay leaves on the surface of the compost. Others push the leaves into the propagating compost obliquely. Perhaps the most obstinate of all the succulents to be propagated in this way is the Aloe, and especially the more thin-leaved types. One can almost guarantee good results, however, with Crassulas, Sedums, and Pachyphytums.

The use of plantlets
A number of Kalanchoes are grown for market which bear little plants on the side of the leaves; these can easily be pulled off with the thumb and forefinger. There is no difficulty in dibbing these into the compost in the propagating frame and they grow very quickly as a rule. *Crassula multicaria* forms plantlets.

The use of offsets

There are succulents which produce baby plants around their bases. It is quite a simple matter to sever these with a sharp knife, half an inch or so below the surface of the soil. The little plantlet, which is called an offset, can then be left for a day to dry out a little before being dibbed into the compost in the propagating box. The authors have on many an occasion severed an offset only to find that it has rooted already in the soil and under these conditions, they have not found it necessary to set the plant in the propagating frame first, but they have been able to pot it up straight away into a little pot containing a compost consisting of 1 part sterilised soil, 1 part coarse silver sand and 1 part sedge peat.

Grafting

One of the sights which fascinated Dr. Shewell-Cooper when he went to study cactus growing in Bordighera on the Italian Riviera was that of thousands of grafted plants in frames. Grafting is a very common method of propagation on the Continent as well as in Britain. It is not as difficult to carry out as many people imagine. However, when grafting some of the species lose their typical characteristics and this is undoubtedly a pity. Some have purposely, for this reason, described grafted plants as freaks—and there is some truth in this.

It would appear that the main reason why commercial growers graft on a big scale is that good saleable plants can be produced far more quickly in this way. The union of the two species appears to be invigorating, but this encouragement to grow usually results in the final plant being not really true to type.

Some have argued that it is necessary to graft some species because they have a tendency to rot off when cuttings are planted at the point where the plant meets the soil. Here one can say that such 'collar rot' may be caused largely through over-watering or because the soil in which the plant was growing was not open enough, or even because there was a little conical depression, however slight, around the base of the plant, in which moisture collected. The answer to this trouble, therefore, need not necessarily be grafting; it can be (a) better compost, (b) more careful watering and (c) the placing of a little collar of finely broken brick around the bottom of the plant so as to make certain that there is aeration here and that moisture cannot collect and cause harm.

Another excuse for grafting is based on the fact that some species have a definite grouping habit of growth and, therefore, if grown in pots, are apt to cascade down over the sides—a fact which does not make them easy to manage. With the *Epiphyllum* group, for instance, one can have, as in the case of the Genus *Zygocactus*, plants which are flattened, forking and much branched and which are commonly called Christmas Cacti. There is also the genus *Schlumbergera*, the plants of which are often called Easter Cacti, which once again have much-branched flat stems with a tendency to be pendant.

One can display to advantage the beauties of the species and hybrids by grafting on to *Pereskia* at whatever height it is desired. It is always said that the *Pereskia* group can be described as a link between ordinary plants and cacti, for their leaves and stems are by no means as succulent as other cacti. *Pereskia aculeata* is the stock most often used.

The columnar types of *Cereus* are also used as stocks, as are species of the *Opuntia*. *Opuntia cylindrica* is sometimes used, for instance, as well as *Opuntia leptocaulis*. It is common in some nurseries to find *Mammillaria angularis cristata* grafted on to *Trichocereus spachianus*.

Readers who would like to attempt grafting should remember that the cut surface of the stock on which the grafting is to take place must be made with a very sharp knife so that it is absolutely flat and smooth. The cut surface of the scion—that is the species or hybrid which is to be grafted on—must also be equally smooth and perfectly level. The idea is that the portion of the cacti forming the scion must rest absolutely level on the cut surface of the cactus forming the stock and it is only in this way that the two may knit together. Of course the ideal thing would be if the area of the stock and scion could be exactly the same size. This, however, is seldom possible.

The species or variety to be grafted should have a surface area smaller than the stock and it can then be placed right in the middle of it and be pegged down in some way. Some have used the long spines of the cacti to push down in between the two to keep them close together; others have engineered special clips, yet others merely tie the graft down to the stock in the best way possible. Some think it a good idea to do the grafting low down so that when the planting takes place in the new pot or border, the species used as the stock can be planted more deeply so that it is hidden, so to speak, by being buried in the soil. The species used as a scion, therefore, is the only one which is seen.

Once again, may we emphasise that it is important to have the two surfaces of the stock and scion absolutely smooth so that they can be fitted together tightly and as the main moisture conducting cells lie towards the very centre of the plants, it is these areas which must be in touch with one another.

There is a more complicated form of grafting by splitting the plant used as a stock longitudinally and then pushing in the scion like a wedge carefully and binding the two together. Amateurs are not likely to use grafting methods at first, but it may be that when they become really proficient in the growing of cacti they may like to try their hand at doing this work, which under certain conditions is by no means too difficult and certainly proves interesting.

Pests which attack cacti and other succulents

Unfortunately, there are a number of insect pests which will attack both cacti and succulents. Many of them go for the plants themselves, above ground, despite the fact that the plants are very thick-skinned. Some, it is true, attack the roots and on the whole these are far more sinister because they are not seen and therefore the beginner has no idea why the plant is looking sickly. Cacti and succulents are not like ordinary plants and one must, therefore, be careful about the insecticides used. It would be tragic indeed to kill the pests if in the process of killing the physical damage done by the remedy proved to be worse than the injury caused by the enemy itself.

Keep your eye on the plants from day to day and be prepared to examine them from time to time with a magnifying glass, because some insect pests like thrips are so small that they are difficult to see with the naked eye. If a plant looks perfectly healthy, then there is little to worry about. If it starts to turn yellow or if any shrivelling is seen; if it starts to flag a little (in the case of the taller branching types); if there are any pits or pock marks—then some serious thought must be given to the subject.

The first thing to determine is whether the trouble is due to insect pests actually attacking the parts of the plant one can see. One must, therefore, make an examination bearing in mind the various insect pests mentioned in this chapter under their separate headings. If no pest can be found, then serious consideration has to be given as to whether the trouble is due to insects attacking the roots. The plant must be turned carefully out of its pot and the root system will be examined even more carefully than the parts above soil level.

Remember, however, that most of the troubles which affect cacti and succulents are due to over-watering. It is true that there are hardly any diseases that make a definite attack and this always h..'ps with the diagnosis of the trouble because it is almost invariably some insect or another. With other plants there are always diseases which may come into the picture and so mask the issue.

The following are the main insect pests which may be found attacking cacti and succulents:

Ants (Formicoidea)

Ants have an unfortunate habit of making their nests in the pots of cacti and succulents. They cause damage to the roots as a result and by their tunnelling may cause excess aeration. They can make a great nuisance of themselves also by transporting mealy bugs and aphides. They carry the aphides about because they want to 'milk' them and so get hold of the honey dew which these creatures exude from their cornicles.

CONTROL MEASURES. Use a product called Nippon. Apply 2 or 3 drops of this on to a piece of wood and stand this on the shelving of the greenhouse or on the window sill of a room. The ants will then come for this 'juice' and will carry it back to their pot nests, where they will use it as food. It will poison all the creatures and in a day or two the trouble will disappear. Nippon is not poisonous to animals or human beings.

A B.H.C. dust is usually effective. In bad cases it may be necessary to knock out the plants after the ants have been killed so as to replace some of the potting soil they will have removed and thus to get rid of the excess aeration.

Mealy bug (Pseudococcus spp.)

The mealy bugs get their name because of the white mealy wax like substance which covers the insects. It is often difficult to find the body of the females despite the fact that they are oval and elongated and about 3 times the size of a pin's head. Actually what you usually see is the mealiness and this is particularly true in the case of the little egg sacs, which are white and woolly. Each female will lay several hundreds of eggs and these hatch out in about 14 days. The little creatures when they first emerge are very active indeed and soon spread over the little plants. It is possible to find mature insects, eggs and babies on cacti and succulents all the year round.

CONTROL MEASURES. Do not spray the cacti and succulents with an oily insecticide. Purchase, however, a small bottle or tin of what is known as a White Oil Emulsion. Any good horticultural chemist will supply this. Use a pointed stick or a child's paint brush and dip this into the emulsion and then place it on the mealy bug itself or the fluffy egg sac in order to remove it. As an alternative Malathion may be used as a spray, but it is important to use it with care and follow the instructions implicitly.

In the case of the root mealy bugs, the plan is to get hold of some crystals of Paradichlorbenzene. Place these on the lower crocks in the pots and the fumes given off by this chemical will kill the insects on the roots. Many people use special perforated zinc coverings to put over the drainage holes of pots. The main use of the perforated zinc is to prevent woodlice from climbing up into the pots.

If the crocks in the pot seem to be infested with root mealy bugs, these should be removed from the base of the plant and should then be scalded with boiling water. The pot, too, should be scalded in this way before it is used again.

Red spider (Tetranychus telarius)
The red spider is, of course, really a mite and for this reason some gardeners purposely call it the red spider mite. The creatures seem to do the greatest amount of damage when the females are feeding ravenously during egg laying time. Infestations are often very severe indeed and the areas thus attacked may appear bleached, or they may be spotted and mottled. They love dry conditions and they can usually be kept under in the case of other plants by syringing regularly with cold water. With cacti, however, this is not advisable.

They are particularly bad pests of Euphorbias, Mesembryanthemums and most types of cacti. They always go for plants which are not growing at their best, possibly because of draughts, imperfect drainage, or lack of sunshine. The eggs which the females lay are spherical and almost impossible to see with the naked eye. The young hatch out as a rule in a week and start sucking the sap. They mate almost immediately and the females then start laying eggs at the rate of 4 a day for about 3 weeks.

When it comes to the late autumn, early winter, red females are produced which have the ability to hibernate.

CONTROL MEASURES. It is fairly easy to kill the red spiders by dusting the plants with very finely powdered Naphthalene Grade 16. This can be dusted on to the cacti or succulents with one of the hand dust guns.

Another method that can be adopted is to spray the plants with a nicotine wash. Dissolve $\frac{1}{4}$ oz (7 gms) liquid nicotine in a $2\frac{1}{2}$-gallon (11·4 lit.) bucketful of water and add a dessertspoonful of a detergent. It is most important to keep down these pests at all times and this is especially so during the hotter, dry months of the year.

Scale insects (Coccidae)
Various scale insects may attack cacti and succulents. These louse-like creatures may be found tightly fixed to the plants and are somewhat troublesome

37   Cacti on display for sale in pots

38   *Neobuxbaumia polylopha*

39   *Oreocereus celsianus*

to eradicate. The hard scaly covering is very typical.

CONTROL MEASURES. Sponging infested plants with a white oil emulsion should help. Alternatively, a pointed stick or brush may be dipped into the emulsion and applied to the plants.

Thrips (Thysanoptera)

These insects are quite inconspicuous. They are never more than a tenth of an inch long; they are usually black in colour and one of the ways of detecting whether they are present on plants is to place a clean white handkerchief on one hand and then tap the pot or plant slightly with a stick to see if any tiny black insects drop on to the white lawn. When looked at under a strong magnifying glass, they appear rather long and thin. The adults may have two pairs of narrow transparent wings. With these they will fly when disturbed from one succulent to another. The baby thrips, however, remain on the plants and continue sucking until they are fully grown. During this process they will exude 'excreta' which causes dry dark spots on the plants and so makes them unsightly.

Twelve generations may occur during the year and it is possible to find the adults, the babies and the eggs on the cacti and succulents all at the same time.

CONTROL MEASURES. Lightly brush infected plants with a Pyrethrum (Pyrethrex) solution. A camel hair paint brush is good for this purpose.

Vine weevil (Otiorrhynchus sulcatus)

It is the grubs of the vine weevil that cause the trouble. They are legless, wrinkled and white and they will be found in the soil partially curled up. Their heads are brown and shiny and they have very strong biting jaws. These grubs hatch out from eggs which may be laid in the crevices of the compost or soil and the hatching will take place in 2 to 3 weeks. From this time onwards the grubs will feed on the roots of the cacti and succulents.

CONTROL MEASURES. When vine weevil grubs are suspected or discovered, the best thing to do is to knock the plants out of the pots, remove the grub or grubs and kill them and then dust the outside of the ball of soil with a 5 per cent. B.H.C. Dust. Infested plants can also be painted with a Pyrethrex solution.

Woodlice (Armadillidium speyeri)

Most people recognise the common woodlouse, which is given all kinds of names in the country, including pea-bug, monkey-bug, pill-bug, sow-bug and slater. These names are used because the woodlice curl themselves up into little balls when they are disturbed. They are grey in colour and have seven pairs of legs and a kind of armour plating body. They usually feed on decaying organic matter, but they are known to attack cacti and succulents and often get into the pots. They should be kept out of these by putting a little perforated zinc covering over the drainage hole. Many horticultural sundriesmen can supply these ready made for the purpose.

CONTROL MEASURES. They may easily be killed by using a Derris dust. This can be applied on the staging of the greenhouse, if that is where the pots of succulents and cacti are standing. It always pays to dust round the walls, heating pipes and supporting pillars.

I I

Fungus diseases

Cacti and succulents are particularly susceptible to diseases caused by fungal infestation. Much can be done to eliminate the risk of infection by the use of properly sterilised soil and care in repotting, since any areas of the plant damaged during this operation will be especially vulnerable to attack.

The two main fungi which attack cacti are *Phytophthera* and *Rhizoctonia* *Fusarium* is also occasionally present. The effects of these fungi are obvious The plant can quite suddenly, seemingly unaccountably, dissolve into a mushy mess.

Unless spotted very early, fungal diseases are nearly invariably fatal to cacti and, since spores can be carried by gnats and other flying insects, affected plants should be removed from small collections at once, even if it means destroying them. It follows therefore that prevention is better than cure.

Prevention of the disease is best done by using properly sterilised soil as mentioned above, and also by correct watering. Incorrect watering, leading to the root ball becoming waterlogged or sodden, will cause the roots to die off through lack of air; similarly if the root ball is unevenly watered, so that dry patches are left (this is particularly likely in early spring when the plants are being started up after their winter rest, and when the soil is hard and compact) the soil may go sour as the roots dry off and this too will result in the appearance of fungi.

Most fungal infestations are combated by drying off the spores with some form of dust or other; however with cacti the diseases nearly invariably start in the watery tissues surrounding the harder core, or stem, of the plant and spread outwards from there. They are often not visible until they have reached the outer surface of the plant by which time the inside is so thoroughly infected that it is no longer practicable to cut out the affected areas. If the disease has reached the central vascular tissues in the core there is seldom any hope left

For this reason most commercial growers prefer to rely on systematic fungicides, that is, fungicides which act through the growing system of the plant and in effect produce a completely sterilised set of tissues in which the fungus is unable to grow. These fungicides however, are not generally available on the market to the amateur and the safest advice is to dip the plants once a month in a solution containing Captan or Karathane in a wettable powder form, during the summer months.

An extended list of cacti, with descriptions

It is our aim in this book to make the general list as simple as possible; however Cactaceae are so numerous and varied that it is best to arrange them under their shapes and sizes on a botanical system of classification. We have used that of Britten and Rose. Although at first sight confusing, even a slight familiarity with the principle will make identification of unlabelled plants much easier. When looking for a known variety we suggest you use the index and turn to the relevant page.

Broadly speaking, cacti are divided into three tribes: Pereskieae, Opuntieae, and Cereeae. The first two are easily distinguished, the Pereskieae being the only Cactus family with persistent leaves just like the leaves on ordinary plants and the Opuntieae being made up of the Prickly Pears which all have glochids —these are little bristly spines tucked into the aerole below the main spine, which adhere readily to fingers and clothing.

Opuntieae and the Cereeae are divided for ease of management into what we might call sub-families depending on their different characteristics; the beginner need only be aware of a few of these. The flat-jointed Opuntias are either *Nopalea*, *Opuntia*, or *Brasilopuntia* (there are others but the beginner is not likely to meet them). Cylindrical Opuntias are *Austrocylindropuntia*, *Cylindropuntia* and *Pterocactus*; those with globular joints are called *Tephrocacti*.

Accordingly, when you want to find a variety look first at its general appearance, whether the joints are flat, cylindrical or globular, then look at the relevant family and see if it is listed. In this way one acquires a more critical eye when looking at the plants.

Cereeae are more complicated and are divided into 8 subtribes, to which the different genera belong; these, broadly speaking, are the Cereanae, Hylocereanae, Echinocereanae, Echinocactanae, Cactanae, Coryphanthanae, Epiphyllanae and Rhipsalidanae.

Cereanae comprise most of the columnar varieties of cacti and mostly grow to a great height, although those you buy in the shop will probably look the same height if not smaller than many of the others. The ribs are arranged vertically and are quite prominent and generally speaking, flowers are not produced until the plant is 18 inches tall, when buds will start to emerge from the sides. Within the group the species may be divided into those with thick stems and those with thin stems the former tending to have more ribs which are less pronounced and appearing in the shops as squat plants rather than the more obviously upright ones.

The Hylocereanae are all night-flowering climbers and produce aerial roots in humid conditions.

The Echinocereanae and Echinocactanae derive the first part of their names from the Greek *echinos*, meaning 'hedgehog'. They are distinguished from the preceding families by their tendency to form low growing clumps and from all other clumping varieties by the absence of pronounced tubercles. They can be distinguished from each other by the way they flower: the Echinocereanae produce buds from the sides of the stems, whereas the Echinocactanae produce buds from the tops of the stems as the spines unfold, the buds being at first concealed among the spines at the tops of the plants.

True Cactanae comprise two genera: *Melocactus* and *Disocactus*. The species of *Melocactus* are rare and difficult to grow; they are characterised by the presence of a woolly cap on top of the older plants.

Coryphanthanae have no ribs, instead they have a number of tubercles arranged spirally. Tubercles are the sort of lumps from which the spines emerge and in this family they are particularly obvious. The Latin word *Mamma* means 'breast'—hence Mammals—and the largest group within the Coryphanthanae is *Mammillaria*, which derives its name from the same Latin word.

The last two sub-tribes are made up of the Leaf Cacti and are arranged as Epiphyllanae and Rhipsalidanae.

The above is a rough guide to the layout of this part of the book and it is hoped that this not only presents a more interesting way of looking at the plants in their natural relation to one another than would a man-made alphabetical order, but also serves as a positive assistance to the beginner attempting to track down a plant which he has bought in a shop, and which is unlabelled. Incidentally, it is often wise to buy unlabelled plants provided you are sure of their quality, since this is an indication of their scarcity—most growers normally only send labelled varieties to the shops when they have enough to justify the expense of ordering a run of labels.

The main groups can be found on the following pages:

	Pages
Pereskieae	74
Opuntieae	75
Cereeae	80
Cereanae	80
Hylocereanae	90
Echinocereanae	92
Echinocactanae	97
Coryphanthanae	112
Epiphyllanae	121
Rhipsalidanae	123

TRIBE No. 1 *PERESKIEAE*

This tribe contains three genera, *Pereskia*, *Rhodocactus* and *Maihuenia*, which are divided into 19 species. These are leafy, shrubby and sometimes vine-like plants, which are used much more as stock for other kinds of cacti such as the *Rhipsalis* and *Zygocactus* than for their own cultivation as ornamental plants. This is a pity because some of them are very free flowering when large and others have very ornamental foliage.

The stems are spiny, not very succulent and often woody. The leaves, which are large and fleshy, are either permanent or sometimes fall during the dormant period. Numerous seeds are produced from the fleshy fruits.

They should be given slightly more shade than normal cacti since full sunlight may scorch the leaves and will certainly turn them yellow.

Pereskia aculeata
HABIT: A vigorous shrub or climber.
HEIGHT: To 30 ft (9 m).
STEMS: Barely succulent, leaves with a prominent midrib, pointed, elliptical.
SPINES: 1–3, hooked, the older ones dark brown and more numerous.
FLOWERS: Whitish, scented. Fruits spiny, yellow.
NOTE: there is also a variety with attractive ornamental leaves—*Pereskia aculeata rubescens*, sometimes known as *P. godseffiana*. The leaves here are a magnificent gold colour, tinged below and on the sides with red.

Pereskia grandifolia
HABIT: Shrubby.
HEIGHT: To 15 ft (4·5 m).
STEMS: Spiny as they become older; leaves pointed at both ends, ovate.

SPINES: At first absent but developing on the older areoles. Black, about 2 in. (5 cm) long when old.
FLOWERS: Pink. The fruit is borne at the top of the stem, is small, green and pear shaped.

TRIBE No. 2 *OPUNTIEAE*

This tribe was one of the first to be described scientifically. The name is pre-Linnaean and is derived from a supposed habitat in Greece. Goethe raised Opuntia seedlings in his home and described them. The tribe has been divided into more than ten genera—*Pereskiopsis, Opuntia, Brasilopuntia, Consolea, Nopalea, Grusonia, Austrocylindropuntia, Cylindropuntia, Tephrocactus* and *Pterocactus* and others. They vary in shape from those with upright cylindrical stems, through the flat jointed ones to some with completely spherical joints, and vary in height from low growing ground cover to large trees.

They are all characterised by the presence of glochids which adhere readily to fingers and clothing. Although neither the spines nor the glochids are poisonous they can cause considerable irritation until they are removed or washed away. The best way to remove the spines is by applying a thin layer of Copydex glue and then rubbing it off so that the spines will come off with it, but soap and water is also a perfectly satisfactory method.

Opuntia aurantiaca (O. extensa)
HABIT: Semi-prostrate and spreading.
HEIGHT: To 5 ft (1·5 m).
STEMS: Joints lanceolate to 10 in. (25·4 cm) long and 1 in. (2·54 cm) wide—dark green.
SPINES: Straight and stiff, to 1 in. (2·54 cm) long, brown to yellow.
FLOWERS: Yellow to 2 in. (5 cm) wide.

Opuntia basilaris (Beavertail Cactus)
HABIT: Low and spreading.
HEIGHT: To 1 ft (91 cm).
STEMS: Thick joints broadly ovate to 7 in. (17·8 cm) long and 4 in. (10·2 cm) wide, bluish green and slightly hairy, sometimes tinged with red.
SPINES: Usually lacking. Areoles recessed, with yellowish brown wool and bristles.
FLOWERS: Dark purple to pink.
NOTE: This variety is very slow growing and must be carefully sheltered from damp during the winter which will cause it to rot off.

Opuntia bergeriana
HABIT: Tall growing, tree-like, with spreading branches.

HEIGHT: To 10 ft (3 m).
STEMS: Trunk to 16 in. (40·6 cm) across. Joints pale green later becoming bluish, 7–10 in. (17·8–25·4 cm) long.
SPINES: Yellowish, awl-shaped, to 2 in. (5 cm) long. Areoles with grey to brownish wool.
FLOWERS: Many on older plants. Orange-red with green six-lobed stigmas.

Opuntia dillenii (O. horrida)
HABIT: Very spiny and thickly branched.
HEIGHT: To 10 ft (3 m).
STEMS: Ovate with irregular margins, 10 in. (25·4 cm) long, thick and grey green.
SPINES: Numerous, to over 2 in. (5 cm) long. Areoles large, yellowish with pale yellow glochids.
FLOWERS: Pale yellow, large to 3 in. (7·6 cm) long.

Opuntia engelmannii
HABIT: Semi-prostrate or erect, branching and growing freely.
HEIGHT: To 5 ft (1·5 m).
STEMS: Joints broadly circular to 12 in. (30·5 cm), thickish, pale green.
SPINES: Mainly white but brown at the base and tip. Areoles bulging outwards with grey wool.
FLOWERS: Yellow, to 3 in. (7·6 cm). Red on the inside.

Opuntia ficus-indica (Indian Fig Cactus)
HABIT: A vigorous grower, erect and tree-like.
HEIGHT: To 15 ft (4·6 m).
STEMS: Oblong joints up to 18 in. (45·7 cm) long, in older plants borne on a cylindrical stem, covered with bluish bloom.
SPINES: Usually absent. Areoles with white wool and yellowish bristles.
FLOWERS: Yellow, to 4 in. (10·2 cm) in diameter.

Opuntia leucotricha (Pl. 35)
HABIT: Upright, tree-like, with numerous branches.
HEIGHT: To 10 ft (3 m).
STEMS: Joints oblong, 4–7 in. (10·2–17·8 cm) long, dark green.
SPINES: To 4 in. (10·2 cm) long, white, flexible. Areoles smallish with yellow glochids and white bristles.
FLOWERS: Yellow, reddish in centre, to 3 in. (7·6 cm) wide.

Opuntia microdasys
HABIT: Erect and spreading bush.
HEIGHT: To 3 ft (91 cm).
STEMS: Joints ovate, pale green, thick, to 4 in. (10·2 cm) long.

SPINES: Usually absent. Areoles close with golden yellow glochids.
FLOWERS: Freely produced, yellow, tinged with red.
This is one of the most popular varieties of cacti but not as harmless as it appears and has given rise to the following cultivars:

Opuntia microdasys albispina (Polka Dots)
Characterised by darker mid-green joints and white glochids, some newer varieties do not lose their glochids when touched.

Opuntia microdasys rufida
Mid-green joints with reddish glochids, not to be confused with Opuntia rufida.

Opuntia microdasys rufida minor (Opuntia rufida minor)
Low-growing, branching with cylindrical ovate joints with reddish glochids.

Opuntia × puberula (O. microdasys × O. cantabrigensis)
This is more hardy than *Opuntia microdasys* and has less closely set areoles, probably the most commonly seen variety.

Opuntia monacantha
HABIT: Tree-like, erect.
HEIGHT: To 7 ft (2·1 m).
STEMS: Joints oblong to oval, narrowed at base; thin, glossy green.
SPINES: Normally solitary, brownish, areoles distant.
FLOWERS: Yellow tinged with red at base.
NOTE: There is a variegated variety *O. m. variegata* in which the young growth is often tinged with pink.

Opuntia robusta
HABIT: As its name implies, vigorous and much branched.
HEIGHT: To 15 ft (4·6 m).
STEMS: Joints large, to 15 in. (38·1 cm), circular, thick, bluish-green.
SPINES: Usually absent in cultivation, occasionally yellow or white. Areoles widely spaced with brown wool.
FLOWERS: Yellow, occasionally tinged with red, to 2 in. (5 cm).

Opuntia tuna
HABIT: Tree-like, erect and quick growing.
HEIGHT: To 12 ft (3·6 m).
STEMS: Joints elliptical, dark green, to 6 in. (15·2 cm) long and 4 in. (10·2 cm) wide.
SPINES: 3–5, to ½ in. (1·3 cm) long, yellowish, spreading. Areoles large with whitish wool and yellow glochids.
FLOWERS: To 4 in. (10·2 cm) wide, yellow, tinged with red.

NOTE: There is also a monstrose variety more commonly seen—*Opuntia tuna monstrosa* which is known as 'Maverick' in the U.S.A. This forms a clump with cylindrical ovate joints, and the areoles bear no spines.

Opuntia vulgaris (Barberry Fig)
HABIT: Prostrate, much branched.
HEIGHT: To 1 ft (30·5 cm).
STEMS: Joints thick, to 4 in. (10·2 cm) long, ovate.
SPINES: Solitary although often absent, stout, to 1 in. (2·54 cm) long. Areoles with grey wool and a few yellowish glochids.
FLOWERS: To 2 in. (5 cm) across, pale yellow.

Brasilopuntia brasiliensis (O. brasiliensis) (Pl. 34)
HABIT: Low growing, bushy, much branching.
HEIGHT: To 2 ft (61 cm).
STEMS: Of two kinds, those on the trunk being circular, those further from the trunk being broadly oblong to elliptical.
SPINES: Few, brownish, flexible, areoles few, with white wool.
FLOWERS: White, plentifully produced on older plants.

Nopalea coccinellifera
HABIT: Erect, slender.
HEIGHT: To 12 ft (3·65 m).
STEMS: Joints long, ovate, pale green and flattened.
SPINES: Usually absent.
FLOWERS: Bright red, to 3 in. (7·6 cm) across with prominent pink stamens.
NOTE: This is one of the host plants for the cochineal scale insect which has been known of since earliest recorded times. It is an easy plant for the amateur and should be included in the collection.

Austrocylindropuntia cylindrica (O. cylindrica)
HABIT: Upright and slightly branched.
HEIGHT: To 10 ft (3 m).
STEMS: Cylindrical, at first with $\frac{1}{4}$ in. (0·6 cm) long leaves which fall in winter. Glossy green.
SPINES: Short, white; areoles recessed with white wool.
FLOWERS: Very small, reddish, appearing just below the ends of the shoots.
NOTE: There is also a cristate form of this from Peru known as *Austrocylindropuntia cylindrica cristata*.

Austrocylindropuntia salmiana (O. salmiana)
HABIT: Upright, bushy, much branched.
HEIGHT: To 3 ft (91 cm).

STEMS: Cylindrical, to ½ in. (1·3 cm) diameter, reddish purple.
SPINES: Up to 5 in number, up to ½ in. (1·3 cm) long, yellowish to grey. Areoles small with many short glochids.
FLOWERS: Yellow, red on the outside.
NOTE: There is a white variety *albiflora*. This is the best *Opuntia* for the beginner who wants to represent this family and have a flowering plant; it will flower when very young.

Austrocylindropuntia subulata (O. subulata)
HABIT: Tree-like with many clustered branches.
HEIGHT: To 5 ft (1·5 cm).
STEMS: Joints cylindrical, tuberculate, dark green, to 2¾ in. (7 cm) thick.
SPINES: 1–2, white, up to 2 in. (5 cm) long. The young shoots produce leaves up to 3 inches long which, unlike *A. cylindrica*, are more persistent. Areoles with only a few yellow glochids on lozenge-shaped tubercles.
FLOWERS: Orange with reddish outside.

Austrocylindropuntia vestita (O. vestita)
HABIT: Upright, sometimes sprawling, many branched.
HEIGHT: To 2 ft.
STEMS: Joints to 8 in. (20·3 cm) long, oblong cylindrical, dark green tuberculate, with light green persistent leaves, up to ½ in. (1·3 cm) long.
SPINES: Numerous, to 1 in. (2·54 cm) long. Areoles yellowish with numerous white glochids and hairs covering the stems.
FLOWERS: Dark red, to 2 in. (5 cm) across.
NOTE: There is a cristate form *Austrocylindropuntia vestita cristata* which is easy to obtain and very pretty.

Cylindropuntia leptocaulis (O. leptocaulis)
HABIT: Compact, bushy.
HEIGHT: To 3 ft (91 cm).
STEMS: Slender and dark green at first, up to 2 in. (5 cm) thick later.
SPINES: Slender, usually solitary, up to 2 in. (5 cm).
FLOWERS: Greenish-yellow, opening only in the morning and evening and closing at mid-day.

Cylindropuntia tunicata (O. tunicata)
HABIT: Prostrate, much branched.
HEIGHT: To 1 ft (30·5 cm).
STEMS: Joints thick, slightly cylindrical, bluish green.
SPINES: 2 in. (5 cm) long, vicious, stiff and barbed with a white papery sheath. Areoles large and white with yellow glochids.
FLOWERS: Yellow 2 in. (5 cm) across.

Cylindropuntia kleiniae
HABIT: Erect and bushy.
HEIGHT: To 8 ft (2·4 m).
STEMS: Joints thick, slightly cylindrical, bluish green.
SPINES: Solitary, to 2 in. (5 cm) long; areoles white with yellowish glochids.
FLOWERS: Purplish, to 1 in. (2·54 cm) in diameter.

Pterocactus kuntzii (P. tuberosus)
HABIT: Much branched with a thick tuberous root stock and numerous prostrate branches direct from the stock.
HEIGHT: To 3 ft (91 cm). Prostrate, to 1 ft (30·5 cm) long.
STEMS: Cylindrical, bluish green to purple, up to 18 in. (45·7 cm) long.
SPINES: 9–12, very small. Areoles small and close.
FLOWERS: Yellow, to 1 in. (2·54 cm) in diameter, at the end of the stems.
NOTE: This variety is often sold as a grafted plant and is best cultivated so, unless really good drainage can be obtained.

TRIBE No. 3 *CEREEAE*

This is the largest tribe within the Cactaceae, and is in turn divided into sub-tribes as outlined earlier. For the beginner with limited space at his disposal they make the best plants.

The descriptions of the various species in this family which follow are based upon plants aged between 2 and 5 years, since this book is meant for beginners and this is the approximate age of the plants that may easily be bought for sale in the shops. This should be borne in mind when comparing descriptions contained here with fuller descriptions based on mature plants in natural conditions in larger works of reference.

Sub-tribe A CEREANAE

This sub-tribe comprises all the species which form tall upright candelabra type plants. The most characteristic of these is the Saguaro—the national flower of Arizona—although the average plant seen in collections which has been pot grown rarely resembles the species as it is found wild. Some of these plants form clumps from the base, others first produce a stem and then branch more like a tree. A more or less distinguishing feature of the whole sub-tribe is, however, the absence of conspicuous joints representing each year's growth such as occur in Opuntias and in certain other types of upright-growing varieties.

The name is derived from the Greek for 'torch'.

One problem confronting the beginner attempting to identify a variety which he has bought in a shop and which has no label is caused by the tendency of most growers to raise their plants for sale from seed. Because this has been the practice for some considerable period, very often hybridisation has occurred between species producing a complete spectrum of plants between two distinct species. This is particularly true in the case of *Cereus peruvianus*, for example; the specimens of which bought in the shops often bear no relation at all to their wild forefathers. If the description nearly fits one variety but differs in the colour of the spines or the number of ribs you may be fairly certain that it is nearly related and that it is probably a hybrid connected with the species.

Cereus jamacaru
Frequently incorrectly sold as *Cereus peruvianus* but differs in having generally more numerous spines and more closely set areoles when young.
HABIT: Erect, upright.
HEIGHT: To 15 ft (4·6 m), but relatively slow growing.
STEMS: Bluish green, becoming greyer with age, with 4–6 prominent ribs.
AREOLES: Round, to ⅜ in. (1 cm) apart when young, later more distant. Numerous radial spines, yellowish brown to ⅛ in. (0·3 cm) long.
FLOWERS: Only produced on mature plants, white, nocturnal.

Cereus peruvianus (Pl. 33)
This is the *Cereus* most commonly seen in collections.
HABIT: Columnar, rarely branching from the base.
STEMS: Bluish green. Ribs 4–5, deeply divided at the top of the plant, less so at the base which may be square to five-sided in section.
SPINES: Brown at base turning to yellow at tip, those on younger plants and at the base of older plants, bristly, becoming stronger with age. About 6 radial spines and 1–4 central spines. Areoles at first close, about 0·2 in. (0·5 cm) apart but later becoming more distant towards the top of the plant (2 cm or more) with grey to greyish yellow felt.
FLOWERS: Seldom occurring on plants less than 12 ft (61 cm) tall, white, nocturnal.

Cereus peruvianus monstruosus (Cereus monstruosus) (Pl. 2)
A monstrose form of the above with much darker stems.

Cereus peruvianus monstrosus minor
A dwarf growing form of uncertain botanical validity. The specimens which we have observed tend to grow slightly faster than the standard *monstruosus* variety.

Cereus aethiops
Best of *Cerei* for flowers. Will flower when only 9 in. (22·9 cm) high.

Monvillea haagei (Pl. 47)
HABIT: Prostrate or semi-erect, frequently grafted, branching.

40 *Cleistocactus straussii*

41 *Stetsonia coryne*

42 *Gymnocalycium mihanovichii 'hibotan'*

43 *Astrophytum ornatum*

STEMS: Green marbled with white at the tip becoming yellower further down, and turning purple nearer the base with age. Ribs at first five becoming four with age, at first low but later becoming more pronounced.

SPINES: 3–4 at first dark brown, later becoming paler, lying close to the stem, the lower one always solitary pointing downwards the remainder always pointing upwards. Areoles 0·2–0·6 in. (0·5–1·5 cm) distant bearing a little grey wool.

FLOWERS: Seldom produced on young plants.

Cephalocereus senilis (Pl. 3)

This species is often known as the Old Man Cactus on account of its long flowing white hair-like bristles. It is very slow growing indeed.

HABIT: Columnar, upright.

STEMS: Mid green, almost completely obscured by the dense covering of bristles. Ribs 12–18 when young, rounded at the edges about 0·2 in. (0·5 cm) high.

SPINES: Weak, white tipped with yellow. On young cultivated specimens these are produced only at the growing tip. Areoles 0·2–0·6 in. (0·5–1 cm) distant bearing a small tuft of white wool and 12–30 long hair-like bristles which ultimately hang down round the plant and give it its aged appearance.

FLOWERS: It is unlikely that the beginner who purchases such a plant as a young specimen will ever see it flower; when produced they are white and nocturnal. The long bristles should be carefully washed in a weak solution of soap and water if they become dirty and if matted. They should then be combed out and the excess soap rinsed off thoroughly. Care should be taken in doing this since the bristly hairs, although coarse are brittle and will break easily.

Cephalocereus palmeri (Pilosocereus palmeri)

HABIT: Columnar, upright, branching when older.

STEMS: Pale to bluish green. 7–8 ribs, rounded.

SPINES: Yellow at first later becoming darker on older plants. 1 central spine about 0·4 in. (1 cm) long surrounded by about 9 radial spines, the shorter ones above, longer below. Areoles about 0·4 in. (1 cm) distant with long fine white bristles 0·4–0·8 in. (1–2 cm) long hanging flat against the stem of the plant along the apex of the rib only.

FLOWERS: Although faster growing than the above species this plant must be of some age to produce flowers. When they are produced they are pale pink, nocturnal and very beautiful.

This plant prefers a slightly more shaded position than other Cereids and should be grown amongst other plants rather than in an exposed situation where it will get full sunlight. It also prefers slightly more warmth in winter during which period it may be better to move it nearer the thermostat if growing in a greenhouse.

Espostoa lanata

This may be at first easily confused with *Cephalocereus senilis* since both are densely covered with white hairs. The hairs on *C. senilis* however are much coarser and longer than *E. lanata* and have a generally more unkempt appearance.

HABIT: Columnar, upright, later branching at the top.

STEMS: More bluish green than in *C. senilis*. Up to 20 low ribs.

SPINES: At first small, bristly, hardly visible between the hairs but immediately apparent on touching. Later 1–2 spines of some length may be produced near the top of the plant, brown at the base, pale in the middle and dark at the tip 0·6–1·2 in. (1·5–3 cm) long and later much longer. Areoles close, 0·2 in. (0·5 cm) apart with fine wool more or less entirely covering the stem up to 0·8 in. (2 cm) long.

FLOWERS: Only produced on mature plants, very small, white.

A form known in the trade as *Espostoa lanata nana* has been seen but appears indistinguishable from the above, though differences can appear in cultivation.

Stetsonia coryne (Pl. 41)

HABIT: Columnar, upright, later branching from the top.

STEMS: Olive green, 9–8 rounded ribs. Central spine 2·4 in. (6 cm) or more long in 3-year-old plants, at first black but later becoming white.

SPINES: Radial spines approximately 10, sometimes 12, depending on the position of the 2 longer spines.

FLOWERS: Green outside, white inside, produced only on mature plants.

The description above is taken from plants circulating in many collections as *S. coryne* but differs from the botanical description of the plant in the absence of V shaped notches above the aeroles and in the far greater number of spines. Another distinguishing feature is the way the spines turn from black to white rather than white to black. It is possible that the species described may properly belong to the *Trichocerei*.

Pachycereus pringlei

HABIT: Columnar, upright, later branching from stem.

STEMS: Mid-green, faintly bluish; Ribs 10–16, prominent.

SPINES: 3 central straw coloured, about 12 radials. Areoles about 0·4 in. (1 cm) apart, slightly woolly.

FLOWERS: Produced only in mature specimens, greenish red outside, white inside.

Pachycereus pecten aboriginum

HABIT: Columnar, upright, later branching from stem.

STEMS: Olive green, ribs 8–12, prominent.

SPINES: Differs from the above *P. pringlei* in having grey central spines later becoming white. Central spines 1–2, radials 10, the lower ones eventually up to 1·2 in. (3 cm) long.

FLOWERS: Produced only in fully grown specimens, reddish outside, white inside.

The name derives from the Latin for 'natives' comb' and apparently refers to the practice of using a cut off rib as a comb.

Eulychnia iquiquensis (floresii)
HABIT: Columnar, upright, branching from base.
STEMS: Dark green, ribs 10–15 low but prominent.
SPINES: Central spine solitary, grey, darker at the tip; radials numerous, hidden amongst the white short wool in the areoles which are practically adjacent in small plants.
FLOWERS: Produced only on older plants, white.
This plant is normally retailed as *E. floresii* which does not appear to be a published name or synonym.

Lemaireocereus pruinosus (now *Ritterocereus pruinosus*)
HABIT: Columnar, upright, occasionally branching.
STEMS: Dull brownish green, bluish at the top. Ribs 5–6, very deep and prominent, slightly spiralled.
SPINES: Central spines usually solitary on younger plants, later up to 4, dark brown later becoming grey. Radial spines 7–9, the same colour. Areoles 0·4 in. (1 cm) apart on young plants, later more distant mounted on knobs on the ribs and with a small amount of white wool in them.
FLOWERS: Produced only on older plants, green and white.
The *Lemaireocerei* as a family are all somewhat delicate and need a little more warmth in winter. *L. pruinosus* is no exception to this and is one of the more delicate; however its very ornamental colouring and form more than reward the care taken over its cultivation.

Lemaireocereus aragonii (now *Marshallocereus aragonii*)
HABIT: Upright, branching from the base.
STEMS: Light green, banded with white meal on some plants, becoming more marked on the lower stem. Ribs 6–8 prominent, slightly rounded.
SPINES: Normally one central spine, at first dark red later becoming grey. Radials 8 although occasionally later more numerous of similar colour. Areoles 0·4–0·6 in. (1–1·5 cm) apart becoming more distant with age, at first with brown felt, later becoming grey.
FLOWERS: Only produced on older plants, red outside white inside.
This species is occasionally incorrectly distributed in the trade as *L. chichipe* from which it differs in having fewer ribs and the grey banding on the stem.

Lemaireocereus thurberi (now *Marshallocereus thurberi*)
HABIT: Columnar, upright, branching from base.
STEMS: Dark olive green subsequently becoming paler with age. Ribs 12–17.
SPINES: Centrals 1–3, at first dark purple later becoming grey, radials 7–9, the same colour. Areoles 0·4 in. (1 cm) apart later becoming more distant, at first with brown or purple wool later becoming grey.
FLOWERS: Produced only on older plants, red outside pink inside.

*Lemaireocereus marginatus (*now *Marginatocereus marginatus)*
HABIT: Columnar, upright, branching from base.
STEMS: Dark green; ribs 5–6, very prominent, edged with purple.
SPINES: Thick and long, 1 or 2 centrals and up to 7 radials. Areoles adjacent with white wool forming a white margin down the ribs of the plant whence it derives its name.
FLOWERS: Produced on older plants only, red and white.

The form most commonly distributed in the shops as L. *marginatus* is in fact *Lemaireocereus marginatus gemmatus (*now *Marginatocereus marginatus gemmatus)* and has much shorter almost insignificant spines.

We have also seen a yellow variety of *Lemaireocereus* purporting to be a form of *Lemaireocereus griseus (Cereus eburneus)*. However, it appears to have fewer radial spines than the type.

Lemaireocereus treleasei (Cereus treleasei, now *Stenocereus treleasei)*
HABIT: Weak, tending to sprawl, occasionally columnar, branching from base.
STEMS: Dark green, 7–9 ribs prominent, rounded.
SPINES: 1–2 centrals at first reddish, later becoming grey tipped with yellow; radials 8–10, the same colour. Areoles about 0·4 in. (1 cm) apart, later up to 0·6 in. (1·5 cm) with short white felt.
FLOWERS: Produced only on older plants, pink.

Wilcoxia schmollii (Echinocereus tuberosus senilis)
HABIT: Weak, sprawling, frequently grafted to advantage, branching from stem.
STEMS: Very dark green, appearing purple, becoming yellow with age nearer the base, 0·4–0·6 in. (1–1·5 cm) thick with 8–10 low ribs. Grafted varieties tend to be only lightly covered with hairs at first, becoming more densely covered as the stem gets older.
SPINES: Weak, bristly. Central spine black at first becoming paler with age, radials white, numerous, becoming hairy with age.
FLOWERS: When grafted this variety produces flowers even when very young. They are a pretty, pale shade of pink with an eight-lobed green stigma. This variety is rapidly becoming more and more available and should be sought for as it is easy to grow when grafted and may be grafted quite easily by taking an obliquely cut section of stem. We have grafted plants with some success onto *Myrtillocactus geometrizans* and *Cereus peruvianus* both of which seem to encourage early flower production.

Nyctocereus serpentinus
HABIT: Upright, fast growing, branching from stem, occasionally jointed especially if growth has been interrupted. Usually requiring a stake.
STEMS: Pale green, becoming yellowish with age. Ribs 10–12, thick and moderately prominent.
SPINES: Weak and bristly, about 7·87 in. (12 cm) long, borne in a cluster from areoles

about 0·2–0·4 in. (5–10 mm) apart. Spines at first white tipped with purple, later becoming more and more white as the purple tip recedes. Areoles small with white felt.

FLOWERS: Reportedly free flowering, although our specimens have taken over five years, pale pink, the inner petals tending to white.

Trichocereus spachianus (T. santiaguensis)

HABIT: Columnar, upright, branching from the base.

STEMS: Mid green becoming yellow with age. Very variable in the number of ribs, generally 10–15. Ribs normally shallow but occasionally more prominent.

SPINES: At first pale yellow later becoming browner finally turning pale with age. Radials 8–10 sometimes more numerous still. Central usually solitary, somewhat longer.

FLOWERS: Produced only on older plants, nocturnal, white.

Trichocereus pasacana

The *Trichocereus pasacana* which we have seen in cultivation exhibit a wide variety of forms most of which seem to be lacking the closely set areoles ascribed by Britton and Rose to this species. While many of them are clearly of hybrid origin and relate to forms of *T. werdemannianus* and *T. terscheckii*, we feel that most of them are probably forms of *T. chiloensis*.

HABIT: Round squat or globular at first only elongating between 4–5 years old, then assuming its natural shape which is upright cylindric and columnar.

STEMS: Pale to dark green, with anything between 11 and 30 ribs which although acute at first become rounded with age. Those with fewer ribs can generally be referred to as *T. werdemannianus*.

SPINES: Very variable especially when the plants are young ranging from white to dark brown. Normally 1–4 central spines surrounded by 8–14 radials which on young plants may be weak becoming stiffer with age, giving the general impression of a well armed cactus. The areoles on most plants sold as *T. pasacana* are too far apart varying from 0·4–0·98 in. (1–2·5 cm), and from brownish yellow to white.

FLOWERS: We have not seen any of the cultivated specimens within this description in flower.

T. werdemannianus has white, closely set areoles, and when young often only six ribs, although these increase with age. *T. pasacana* also has closely set areoles but has more ribs and seldom fewer than ten. *T. terscheckii* has areoles 0·8–1·2 in. (0·2–0·3 cm) apart and typical plants have 8 to 14 ribs, and yellowish areoles. *T. chiloensis* has the same number of ribs but has white areoles with a slight notch above them on the rib which is visible even in young plants.

Within *T. chiloensis* the following varieties have been recorded:
var. *eburneus*, white spines.
var. *spinosissimus*, brown spines directed upwards.
var. *panohopkitas*, young spines almost black.

We have also seen plants of *T. werdemannianus* and *T. pasacana* which are probably referable to *T. poco* which when young has long needle-like spines at first dark brown becoming yellow with age forming a fairly dense covering over the plant.

Carnegiea gigantea

Young plants sold in pots differ markedly from most published pictures of this plant, which is the native flower of Arizona, attaining great age and height there. Horticultural specimens of less than six years might easily be mistaken for something else altogether since they are round and globular rather than upright and cylindrical. They are extremely slow growing and unlikely to flower in cultivation. Interesting only on account of their associations.

HABIT: When young, globular, only elongating and becoming upright when fairly old. Seldom exceeding a few feet high in cultivation, very slow growing.
STEMS: Mid green, when young with about 11 ribs.
SPINES: Radials 11 or more in number, white tipped brown. Centrals 4–5 brown when young becoming paler from the tip downward with age. Areoles on young plants to 1 cm apart somewhat woolly when young.
FLOWERS: White. Unlikely in cultivation.

Oreocereus celsianus

The plants sold under this name in fact are normally referable either to *O. celsianus* or *O. fossulatus*. From the descriptions which follow, they can be distinguished.
Oreocereus celsianus (Pl. 39)
HABIT: Upright, columnar, branching from low down.
STEMS: Mid- to grey-green with between 9 and 17 ribs, prominent, rounded and notched above the areole.
SPINES: Radials completely hidden beneath the hair; Centrals 1–4 brownish yellow protruding through the hairs. Areoles about 0·4 in. (1 cm) apart when young, developing enormous quantities of long silky white hairs which form a dense mass on top of the stem and hang down for some distance.
FLOWERS: Seldom produced in cultivation under glass, reddish.

Oreocereus fossulatus

HABIT: Upright, columnar, branching from low down.
STEMS: Generally more sturdy than *O. celsianus* with 9–14 prominent ribs, more deeply notched than the preceding species and slightly darker green.
SPINES: Thicker and sturdier than *O. celsianus*, with approximately 11 radials and 1–4 centrals, a strong golden brown becoming straw coloured with age. Areoles much larger than the preceding species up to 0·8 in. (2 cm) apart, with conspicuous white felting and producing long silky hairs similar to *O. celsianus* but in less profusion and without the matted appearance of the former.
FLOWERS: Seldom produced in cultivation under glass, larger and redder than the preceding species.

O. fossulatus was formerly regarded as a variety of *O. celsianus* which accounts partly for the fact that it is often labelled as *O. celsianus*.

O. trollii differs from *O. celsianus* in having a rounder stem at the base and fewer ribs.

Cleistocactus baumannii

HABIT: Upright, columnar, branching freely from the base.
STEMS: Pale green, 10–15 low ribs.
SPINES: Densely covering the stems, at first brown tipped with yellow, later becoming greyish. Centrals 1–4 much longer much thicker and broader than the radials. Areoles 0·4 in. (1 cm) distant with greyish felt.
FLOWERS: Flowers produced freely on plants 7 years old and more from woolly areoles at the tips, orange-scarlet.

Cleistocactus straussii (Pl. 40)

HABIT: Upright, columnar, sending up offsets from the base.
STEMS: Mid-green, 23–25 narrow low ribs.
SPINES: Almost hidden amongst the long white hairs produced from each areole. About 4 in number, pale yellow. Areoles small with white wool about 5 mm apart. In some forms the spines may be white.
FLOWERS: Produced only on older plants, 2–3 ft (60·5–91 cm) high, red, tubular.

Many of the plants offered for sale as *C. straussii* are in fact *C. straussii* var. *jujuyensis*. They can be differentiated by their longer spines and fewer hairs. The spines are pale yellow to brown and clearly visible.

Lophocereus schottii

HABIT: Upright, columnar, branching from the base.
STEMS: Pale olive green, slightly pruinose, becoming greyish with age. The growing tips are normally tinged a deep shade of purple and this persists round the younger areoles. Five to 7 prominent ribs slightly notched above the areoles.
SPINES: Brittle and irregular in appearance; generally 5 but occasionally on young growth solitary, while older plants may have up to 7. Areoles about 0·4–0·6 in. (1–2 cm) distant with a small amount of greyish hair between the base of the spines.
FLOWERS: Produced only after a considerable number of years on mature plants as this is a slow growing variety, green outside, red inside.
NOTE: There is a montrose form which is now popular. It is spineless and called the Totem Pole Cactus.

Myrtillocactus geometrizans

HABIT: Upright, columnar, freely branching from the sides of the stem 6 in. (15 cm) up.
STEMS: Very impressive, thick in later life although thin when young, pale bluish green, banded slightly with the new growth. Darker green round the areoles. Ribs 5–6, very broad.

SPINES: Young plants produce 3 short black spines 0·04–0·07 in. (0·1–0·2 cm) long from the areoles, but older plants produce one central spine up to 1·2 in. (3 cm) or more in length with up to 5 radials, all black at first becoming grey with age and easily broken off. Areoles distant, even on young plants, 0·59–1·57 in. (1·5–4 cm).
FLOWERS: Small, produced from the upper areoles of well established plants of considerable age.

Although regularly used as grafting stock, this variety is not really suitable for this purpose since it requires considerably higher temperatures in winter. This species has a tendency to produce brown necrotic patches at the sides of the stems. We have not been able to ascertain the exact nature of these but they are clearly associated with cold weather during winter; plants grown in warmer houses seldom exhibit them. We suggest a minimum winter temperature of 10°C (50°F). If desired the brown patches may be removed with a scalpel or a sharp razor.

Myrtillocactus schenkii
HABIT: Upright, columnar, branching from stem.
STEMS: Olive green, paler at the growing tips with 6–8 ribs, prominent and broad.
SPINES: One central spine at first 0·2 in. (0·5 cm) long later up to 2 in. (5 cm), brown. 5–7 radials of similar colour. Areoles with brownish grey felt about 0·27 in. (0·7 cm) apart when young later becoming more distant.

Sub-tribe B   HYLOCEREANAE
The members of this sub-tribe are all climbing or sprawling plants frequently making aerial roots if given the chance. They all have magnificent flowers, most of them produced at night, and fairly freely on plants five years of age and older.

We suggest that they are planted out in a greenhouse against a wall wherever possible as this seems to give the best results. If it is desired, however, to retain them in pots we suggest that they be given something to climb up, either a mossed stick or a piece of bark, and be encouraged to root into this.

Neobuxbaumia polylopha (Pl. 38)
HABIT: Solitary, branching only when older.
HEIGHT: To 2·4–2·8 in. (6 or 7 cm) after 3 years but growing much taller in the wild.
STEMS: Pale green with 12–15 prominent broad ribs.
SPINES: Radials, straw coloured, about 7, pointing downwards to 0·4 in. (1 cm) in length. Centrals solitary, straw coloured to 0·4 in. (1 cm) in length, becoming paler with age. Areoles very slightly woody.
FLOWERS: Produced only on older plants.

Hylocereus trigonus
HABIT: Sprawling or climbing, branching freely along the stem.

STEMS: Jointed, pale green normally with 3 very prominent ribs with acute edges, but sometimes triangular in section and chunky.
SPINES: 1–3 lower radials which are white and bristly, remaining spines 3–6 brownish to brownish yellow. Areoles 0·4 in. (1 cm) apart, the ribs deeply notched above them.
FLOWERS: Large and white, produced on older plants.

Hylocereus undatus is differentiated from this by its short thick spines and the absence of the bristles. *H. trigonus* is, however, frequently supplied under the name of *H. undatus*.

Selenicereus grandiflorus
HABIT: Climbing, much branched.
STEMS: Light green becoming purple with age, 5–7 low ribs.
SPINES: At first yellowish, later turning grey with age; 7–11 borne on areoles 0·4–0·6 in. (1–1·5 cm) apart with pale yellow wool and at first with golden wool which later disappears with age.
FLOWERS: Borne from ripened stems on plants which have become well established. Very large, white and heavily scented.

This species is known in England as 'Queen of the Night'. *S. pteranthus*, 'Princess of the Night', is reputedly hardier than *S. grandiflorus* and has angled stems rather than ribbed ones.

Selenicereus boeckmannii
Sometimes considered to be a hybrid between the two preceding species.
HABIT: Climbing, branching freely.
STEMS: Light green becoming yellow or purple with age, 5–7 low ribs.
SPINES: Borne in clusters, the outer ones white and spreading, the inner ones yellowish and pointing outwards. Areoles white felted about 0·27 in. (0·7 cm) apart.
FLOWERS: White, heavily scented, produced even in fairly young plants.

Aporocactus flagelliformis (syn. *Heliaporus smithii*)
HABIT: Creeping or hanging, often grafted to advantage.
STEMS: At first bright green but becoming greyer with age; 10–14 low ribs.
SPINES: Borne in star-like clusters of 15–20 at first with a red tinge to them but later becoming straw coloured. Areoles close, 0·2 in. (0·5 cm) apart, with white to grey felt.
FLOWERS: Very freely produced, bright red.

This variety and the next one both require full sunlight at all times and may be watered even during the winter. The stems tend to rot back with age which can cause the plant to die, so it is a very good idea to graft them either onto a strong *Hylocereus* stock or, more usually, onto *Selenicereus*.

Aporocactus mallisonii [X *Heliaporus mallisonii (smithii)*]
HABIT: Generally similar to *A. flagelliformis*, of which it is a hybrid crossed with

Heliocereus speciosus. This accounts for its stronger more robust growth and means it may be more readily grown on its own roots.

Sub-tribe C ECHINOCEREANAE

The two previously discussed sub-tribes have all had cylindrical stems of some length and size. The Echinocereanae, however, are clump forming and although they have cylindrical stems these are seldom very tall. They are all easy to flower and certain varieties such as *Setiechinopsis mirabilis** and certain Rebutias will flower when barely a year old. This free flowering even when very young is an important distinguishing feature for the amateur. The flowers are produced from the sides of the stem and the presence of buds is indicated either by an areole starting to produce large quantities of wool as in the *Echinocerei* or by the presence of minute red buds in the lower areoles as in *Rebutia* and *Aylostera*.

In order to obtain the maximum number of flowers from a plant within this group it is best to wait until the red buds or woolly areoles are clearly visible before giving them any water. However, if there is no sign of buds by April there may either be something wrong with the plant, or it may not be sufficiently established to flower, or it may not have been kept dry enough during the winter.

Echinocereus salm-dyckianus
HABIT: Stiff, semi-erect, short, branching freely from base.
STEMS: Light green with 7 slightly prominent ribs.
SPINES: 1–3 centrals greyish yellow, darker at the tips. 9 radials the same colour. Areoles close, 0·2 in. (0·5 cm) apart, yellow felted later becoming brown.
FLOWERS: Not at first very freely produced although the species is fast growing, orange.

Echinocereus viridiflorus
HABIT: Stiff, semi-erect, short, branching from the base.
STEMS: Green with 11–13 spirally arranged ribs.
SPINES: About 15, dark red at first turning yellow, very small. Central spine often absent, particularly on grafted specimens. Areoles close, about 0·2 in. (0·5 cm) apart normally, with white felt.
FLOWERS: Green in colour.

This species is extremely variable in its habit and the above is intended more as a general description of the varieties we have seen offered for sale under this label and which can be referred to the true species.

* Now belongs to the Cereanae family.

Echinocereus pentalophus
HABIT: Prostrate, freely branching, forming a clump from the base.
STEMS: Pale green with 4–5 warty ribs.
SPINES: 4–5 radiating, star-like, 0·8 in. (2 cm) in length or more. Areoles 0·6 in. (1·5 cm) apart on raised warts on the ribs, white at first becoming grey with age.
    Echinocereus procumbens may be a variety of this with longer stems and darker flowers.

Echinocereus rigidissimus
HABIT: Usually small, solitary, seldom more than 11·8 in. (30 cm) high.
STEMS: Mid-green with 12–23 ribs, low and blunt.
SPINES: Short, spreading and white, brown at the base and darker at the tip. 16–22 spreading starlike from the areoles and completely covering the plant, the tips of the spines appearing to form an extra ridge where they join. Centrals absent; areoles adjacent, oval, white.
FLOWERS: Pink, produced on 3-year-old plants and older.
    E. rigidissimus was formerly regarded as a variety of *E. pectinatus* and the *E. pectinatus* of horticulture is often in fact *E. rigidissimus*. *E. pectinatus* differs in having 2–3 central spines and in its tendency to branch more freely from the base.

Echinocereus fitchii (Pl. 8)
HABIT: Very variable, upright, branching from the base in later life.
STEMS: Dark green, frequently tinged purple with 13 broad prominent ribs.
SPINES: About 20, short, radiating, white tipped purple. Central spines usually single and completely purple when young. The spine colour is very variable in the plants sold by growers under this label and clearly a wide range of hybridisation has occurred. Areoles about 0·2–0·4 in. (0·5–1 cm) apart, slightly brown.
FLOWERS: Magnificent, freely produced from woolly areoles at the top of the stem, brilliant pink up to 3·54 in. (9 cm) in diameter. Flowers well even when young.

Echinocereus enneacanthus
HABIT: Semi-erect, spreading, forming clumps from the base.
STEMS: Pale green with seven prominent ribs, warty, broad, rounded.
SPINES: Yellow becoming white with age; 7–9 radials spreading with usually one central but occasionally more. Areoles 0·4–0·6 in. (1–1·5 cm) apart, felted white, often with horizontal furrows on the ribs above them.
FLOWERS: Red, less freely produced than in the foregoing species.
    There is also a cristate variety which appears to be quite widely available, but is not particularly remarkable.

Echinocereus stramineus (Cereus stramineus)
HABIT: Erect, forming clumps from plants about three to four years old.
STEMS: Light green with 9–13 low, broad, rounded, warty ribs.

SPINES: At first brown becoming white with age. Central spines 1·2–3·5 in. (3–9 cm) long, 1–3 in number. Radials 7–10, apparently always white on cultivated specimens. Areoles 0·6 in. (1·5 cm) apart, with white felt.

FLOWERS: Not very freely produced, purple.

There is also a variety which we have seen with pure white spines occasionally red at the base when young.

Rebutia (Pl. 31–32)

The Rebutia normally offered for sale in pots are a complex mixture of different varieties resulting from intense cross-hybridisation, both natural and man-inspired, between three varieties. We consider that the horticultural varieties are of such abundance and variety that only a broad outline of the major differences is likely to be of any help to the beginner seeking to identify a particular plant. However, although their parentage may be a matter of doubt their potential and value in a collection cannot be over-emphasised. The majority flower when only one year old and produce an enormous variety of colours.

HABIT: All Rebutias are clump forming, and most are globular. R. *pygmaea* discussed in more detail below, is an exception and R. *senilis* tends to become cylindrical with age.

STEMS: Globular with tubercles arranged spirally around the plant in anything from 20 rows—R. *minuscula*; to 25 or more in the case of R. *violaciflora*.

SPINES: Extremely variable in colour and number. R. *senilis* has long white silky spines, more like hairs or bristles which form a dense covering on the plant. R. *violaciflora* produces anything from 3–5 central spines and the true R. *minuscula* of botanists has a solitary central spine. The colour in the last two species varies from a yellowish white to a fairly deep brown. Areoles are arranged on tubercles in a spiral formation and are generally fairly close, seldom more than 0·4 in. (1 cm) apart, they usually produce white felt but this can be any shade towards a brownish yellow.

FLOWERS: Probably as a result of hybridisation these are the most variable characteristic of all. We have seen white, pinks, lilacs, violets, reds, oranges and yellows. Attempts have been made to give some of these Latin varietal names such as R. *senilis* var. *stuemeriana* which, unlike the true R. *senilis*, has a much more orange throat, the species having a red flower. However, we have observed plenty of plants which when not in flower accord well with the description of R. *senilis* and which subsequently have produced clear yellow flowers.

Generally speaking the globular Rebutias are of the easiest cultivation and can be flowered without difficulty in the house on a sunny windowsill. In order to produce flowers, however, they must be kept dry from about September until March when red buds usually start to appear round the old areoles near the base of the plant. Give a little water when these appear and move them into a warmer room, but do not give any further water until you are sure they are buds (that is to say, until they are about 0·07–0·1 in. (2–3 mm) long and still quite red with no sign of green) and not just new offsets.

Rebutia pygmaea (Mediolobivia pygmaea) (Pl. 21)
HABIT: Short, stumpy, slightly cylindrical, slow growing, branching.
STEMS: Dark green with tubercles arranged in up to 10 slightly spiral rows.
SPINES: Very small on cultivated plants seldom exceeding 0·1 in. (3 mm) in length, whitish about 10 in number and clinging close to the stem. No centrals.
FLOWERS: Red with rounded petals freely produced on the sides of the stem.

R. *pygmaea* has changed its name so often that it may be as well to list some of the genera into which it has wandered—*Lobivia, Echinopsis, Mediolobivia* and even *Pygmaeolobivia*. As *Pygmaeolobivia haagei* it should not be confused with either *Lobivia haageana* or *Rebutia haagei*, two distinct species with larger spines.

Aylostera spegazziniana
HABIT: Cylindrical forming clumps from the base.
STEMS: Dark glossy green with 11–13 rows of tubercles arranged slightly spirally.
SPINES: Very.short, white sometimes tipped brown. Central spines occasionally present. Areoles small, white, spineless when young about 0·4 in. (1 cm) apart.
FLOWERS: Orange with a yellowish throat produced round the sides of the stem.

Similar confusion seems to exist amongst the plants of *A. spegazziniana* and *A. deminuta* which are offered for sale by growers. *A. deminuta* differs in that it is more globular in habit. Some textbooks refer all varieties of *Aylostera* to *Rebutia*.

Aylostera deminuta (Pl. 10)
HABIT: Low, forming clusters from the base.
HEIGHT: To 6 in. (15·24 cm).
STEMS: Dark green, slightly greyish with about 13 spirally arranged rows of tubercles.
SPINES: Radials 8–10, white, tipped brown. Centrals usually absent. Areoles about 1 cm apart with a little brown felt.
FLOWERS: Fiery orange, very freely produced.
Aylostera pseudodeminuta (Pl. 9) is very similar.

Lobivia
These are not so commonly sold as they should be, since they are very variable in flower colour and easily raised from seed. On the whole they look like very large Rebutias and require similar treatment. The flowers are short and funnel-shaped or bell shaped, red, pink, pale orange or apricot.

Lobivia densispina (L. famatimensis)
A very variable species having many horticultural varieties.
HABIT: Either solitary or occasionally forming clusters.
HEIGHT: To 3–4 in. (7·6–10·2 cm).
STEMS: Dark green, somewhat purplish, but mainly covered by the spines. Ribs, 20 or more, low.
SPINES: Very variable in colour and size, normally white or straw coloured, com-

pletely covering the stem. Areoles close, ¼ in. (0·6 cm) apart.

FLOWERS: Of every hue of red, pink and orange, produced from woolly buds on the side of the plants.

Lobivia jajoiana

HABIT: Globular, forming clumps.

HEIGHT: To 3 or 4 in. (7·6 to 10·2 cm).

STEMS: Frequently purplish occasionally dark green with 12 to 15 notched ribs.

SPINES: Radials 9–12, short, brown becoming grey with age. Centrals 1–3 the longest up to 1½ in. (3·8 cm) in length, hooked.

FLOWERS: Brilliant red, very beautiful, produced nearer the top of the stems than in the preceding species.

There are many other varieties of *Lobivia* but the above two are the ones most frequently found in cultivation. Of them we recommend *Lobivia pentlandii* which is fairly free flowering and not uncommon in cultivation.

Pseudolobivia kratochvilleana (Echinopsis kratochvilleana) (Pl. 28)

HABIT: Globular, to hemispherical.

HEIGHT: To four inches.

STEMS: Pale to mid-green with 15 or more narrow ribs.

SPINES: Radials 10, grey, weak and somewhat bristly. Centrals stouter, 1–2 in number and up to 1 in. (2·54 cm) long.

FLOWERS: Produced on a long tube from the upper areoles, very beautiful white, occasionally flushed pink.

Pseudolobivia aurea (Lobivia aurea)

HABIT: Globular at first, elongating with age.

HEIGHT: To 5 in. (12·7 cm).

STEMS: Pale green with about 15 ribs.

SPINES: Radials 6–10, grey or purple tipped dark, Centrals 1–4 up to 1 in. (2·54 cm) in length.

FLOWERS: Yellow produced from the upper areoles, very beautiful.

This species is extremely variable and as the result of hybridisation and selection by nurserymen a complete range of plants between *Lobivia famatimensis* and *P. aurea* seems to be available.

Echinopsis multiplex

HABIT: Globular at first, becoming cylindrical with age and making many offsets.

HEIGHT: To 6 in. (15·24 cm).

STEMS: Pale green with 12–14 sharp straight ridges.

SPINES: Radials variable normally about 10, straight, yellowish with dark tips. Centrals about 4, curved, darker. Areoles distant to 1 in. (2·54 cm) apart, spreading.

FLOWERS: This species is not very free flowering and needs very harsh treatment and a long period of drought if it is to flower. The flowers are borne at the end of a long tube from the side of the plant, pale pink, sweet smelling.

Echinopsis eyriesii is frequently sold under the above name but is distinguished by having fewer ribs and more reddish spines. The flowers are white. However, hybridisation has occurred between all these types of *Echinopsis* species and it may be very difficult to fit an acquired specimen into one of the descriptions.

Echinopsis rhodotricha
Another extremely variable species, at first easily mistaken for a *Trichocereus*.
HABIT: At first solitary forming clumps when 5 years old.
HEIGHT: To 2½ ft (76 cm).
STEMS: Dark to mid green with 8–13 straight ribs.
SPINES: Radials 4–7, curved, brown yellow or even white. Centrals usually solitary of variable length and colour, sometimes lacking altogether.
FLOWERS: Produced somewhat reluctantly in cultivation and only on older plants. White.

Setiechinopsis mirabilis (Pl. 27)
HABIT: Solitary, branching occasionally from the base.
HEIGHT: To 4 in. (10 cm) but seldom achieving this.
STEMS: Brownish-purple in colour with 12–14 shallow ribs slightly notched around the aeroles.
SPINES: Radials about 10, 2–5 mm in length, white tipped with brown. Centrals solitary, 0·8 in. (2 cm) at first appearance black, becoming grey tipped with brown. Areoles close, slightly woolly.
FLOWERS: Nocturnal, white, slightly scented at the end of a long tube.
NOTE: The plant usually dies after two years but fresh plants may be raised easily from the seed.

Sub-tribe D   ECHINOCACTANAE
One of the most important distinguishing features of this group of cacti is the way in which the flowers are always produced with the new areoles at the top of the plant. In *Parodia* the presence of flowers buds can be detected fairly early on towards the end of January in some species by the presence of a thick wad of bristly hairs between the spines and in some other varieties such as *Noto-cactus* and *Gymnocalycium* the buds appear among the spines and only become really prominent later in life.

Water should be given as soon as the weather begins to get warmer towards the middle or end of April and the buds should be clearly developed on most species about a month after this. However, care should be taken with *Parodia* many of which flower later in the year and some of them such as *Parodia gracilis* may not flower until it is almost winter.

Parodia

These are only just starting to be made available in large numbers and because of the ease with which they may be flowered should be bought by every collector. More and more varieties come onto the market every year and careful selection from *P. chrysacanthion* through to *P. gracilis* will ensure something in flower from March to October.

We propose to divide them into two groups for ease of identification; those with unhooked central spines and those with hooked spines.

The following two varieties are with unhooked spines:

Parodia chrysacanthion (Pl. 26)
HABIT: Globular, occasionally subcylindrical.
HEIGHT: To 3 in. (7·6 cm).
STEMS: Pale green with about 30 low ribs slightly tubercled.
SPINES: Radials dense, numerous, weak, bristly, white or straw coloured, to 1½ in. (3·8 cm) long. Centrals to 2 in. (5 cm) long golden yellow when young, may become white with age. Areoles close at first with pale yellow wool which later disappears.
FLOWERS: Produced in early spring amongst the spines at the top, small, yellow.

Parodia nivosa
HABIT: Globular.
HEIGHT: To 3 in. (7·6 cm).
STEMS: Dark green, young plants have nine spiral rows of tubercles but older plants may have many more.
SPINES: Radials 13–14, white to 0·4 in. (1 cm) long. Centrals usually solitary in horticulturally produced plants, 3–5 in imported ones, white at first becoming brown with age. Areoles large with conspicuous white hair.
FLOWERS: Red produced on older plants of at least 3 years old.

The following varieties all have at least one hooked spine:

Parodia microsperma (Pl. 25)
HABIT: Globular, forming clumps.
HEIGHT: To 3 in. (7·6 cm).
STEM: Pale green almost hidden by spines borne on 22 or more spirally arranged rows of tubercles.
SPINES: Radials, 9–13 spreading, white to 1 in. (2·54 cm) long, Centrals 3–4 reddish the longest up to 1½ in. (3·8 cm) long, hooked. Areoles to ¼ in. (0·6 cm) apart at first with white wool, later without.
FLOWERS: The true species has red outer petals with orange inner petals but horticultural plants exhibit a wide variety of colours, from red to yellow and many appear to have been crossed with *P. rubellihamata*.

Parodia rubellihamata
HABIT: Globular.
HEIGHT: To 3 in. (7·6 cm).
STEM: Mid green with 20 low spiral ribs.
SPINES: Radials about 20 in number, to ½ in. (1·3 cm) long, white at first becoming grey with age, weak. Centrals 3, brownish red tipped with black when young, the longest hooked and up to 1 in. (2·54 cm) or more in length. Areoles at first woolly, white, to ¼ in. (0·6 cm) apart, later losing the wool.
FLOWERS: Again there is a variety here in the horticulturally produced specimens varying from red to yellow, the true species has yellow flowers.

Parodia maassii
HABIT: Upright at first and almost cylindrical.
HEIGHT: To 6 in. (15·2 cm) but slow growing.
STEM: Pale to mid green with 23 low spiralled ribs.
SPINES: Radials 9, straw coloured, Centrals 3 to 1½ in. (3·8 cm) in length, the longest hooked at the end and pointing downwards with age, dark brown. Areoles to ½ in. (0·4 cm) apart with brown felt.
FLOWERS: Produced only on older plants.

Parodia scopaoides
HABIT: Globular
HEIGHT: To 3 in. (7·6 cm).
STEMS: Dark green with tubercles arranged in 25–30 ribs completely hidden by the spines.
SPINES: Radials, numerous, spreading, white to 1 in. (2·54 cm) in length. Centrals 3–5 stouter red tipped black to 1 in. (2·54 cm) hooked. Areoles close, to 5 mm apart at first with white wool, later becoming yellowish and losing the wool.
FLOWERS: Reddish orange.

Parodia mairanana
HABIT: Globular.
HEIGHT: To 3 in. (7·6 cm).
STEMS: Pale to mid green with 13 or so spiral broad ribs notched deeply horizontally under each areole.
SPINES: Radials 7–9 greyish yellow tipped black to 1 in. (2·54 cm) long. Centrals 3–4 the same colour, the longest hooked and up to 1½ in. (3·8 cm) in length. Areoles at first woolly to ½ in. (1·2 cm) apart.
FLOWERS: Orange.

Parodia sanagasta
HABIT: Globular.
HEIGHT: To 3 in. (7·6 cm).

STEMS: Grey green, occasionally reddish with 20–25 spiral broad, slightly tuberculate ribs.

SPINES: Radials 13, grey, tipped purple, to ¾ in. (1·9 cm) in length. Centrals at first dark purple, 3–4 in number, the longest hooked and up to 1 in. (2·54 cm) in length, later becoming greyer with age. Areoles grey, to ½ in. (1·3 cm) apart, at first slightly woolly.

FLOWERS: Yellow.

Parodia sanguiniflora (Pl. 23)

HABIT: Globular.

HEIGHT: To 4 in. (10·2 cm).

STEMS: Dark green with numerous spiral tuberculate ribs.

SPINES: Radials 12–15, white, weak to 1 cm in length. Centrals 3–4, brownish the longest up to 1 in. (2·54 cm) in length and hooked at the tip. Areoles close about 0·2 in. (0·5 cm) apart, very woolly at first.

FLOWERS: Produced in great profusion in early summer, blood red.

Parodia gracilis (Pl. 24)

HABIT: Globular.

HEIGHT: To 4 in. (10·2 cm).

STEMS: Pale green with 16 low ribs.

SPINES: Radials 20 or more, white with brownish tips, to 1 in. (2·54 cm) in length. Centrals 4–5, brown at first becoming white with age. Areoles about ½ in. (1·3 cm) apart, large, felted.

FLOWERS: Orange, small, produced among the spines at the top right into winter. A very worthwhile plant on account of this.

Parodia rubriflora

HABIT: Similar to *Parodia sanguiniflora* but generally smaller in all its parts. It may in fact be a horticultural variety of *P. sanguiniflora*.

Parodia mutabilis

HABIT: Globular.

HEIGHT: To 3 in. (7·6 cm).

STEMS: Bluish green with several spirally arranged rows of tubercles.

SPINES: Radials, dense and very numerous although somewhat weak, usually white, although some plants sold under this name which are probably hybrids tend to have straw coloured radials. Centrals 3–4 ranging in colour from white to orange, those with orange centrals being probably the most characteristic.

FLOWERS: Yellow or occasionally orange.

Parodia aureispina

HABIT: Globular.

HEIGHT: To 3 in. (7·6 cm).

STEMS: Pale to mid green with spiral ribs notched and tuberculate.
SPINES: Radials numerous thin, weak and white. Centrals up to six in number and up to 1 in. (2·54 cm) in length, golden yellow. Areoles close to 0·2 in. (0·5 cm) apart. Tawny yellow.

There is a similar variety in cultivation under the name of *Parodia aurihamata* which is extremely difficult to distinguish. The varieties named *P. aurihamata* which we have seen have had yellow flowers without any tinge of orange in them. *Parodia aureispina* itself is somewhat rare and most varieties offered for sale as such are probably hybrids involving *P. mutabilis* and *P. aurihamata*.

Malacocarpus erinaceus (now *Wigginsia erinaceus*)
HABIT: Globular.
HEIGHT: To 4 in. (10·2 cm).
STEMS: Dark green with 15–20 broad ribs with wavy edges.
SPINES: Radials up to 8 in number, at first brown but becoming grey with age. Centrals solitary up to 1 in. (2·54 cm) in length the same colour. Areoles about 0·6 in. (1·5 cm) apart produced in the notches in the ribs, at first with white wool.
FLOWERS: Yellow, similar to *Parodia*. We have been unable to flower this plant with any degree of certainty at less than four years old, but once it has reached this age it seems to flower with some ease.

Notocactus

Notocactus species are very commonly seen in shops and are probably more frequently found in small collections than any other type. In spite of this we have seen a surprisingly large number of poorly grown specimens whose full flowering potential has never been realised. It is advisable in order to flower these fine plants that they be kept absolutely dry from September to March. At Rochfords we keep our plants of *N. submammulosus* var. *pampeanus* and *N. tabularis* dry for one month longer than any other type of cactus and in this way we are able to produce up to four buds on the former and up to three on the latter even when they are only two years old. Like *Parodia* they are coming in for a lot more attention from growers since there are varieties with exotic colours such as the purple *N. herteri* which should be generally available for sale in a few years although comparatively rare at the moment and the newer Parodia-like ones such as *Notocactus horstii* which seems to go on and on producing flowers even during the winter when it should otherwise be resting. Their main drawback is that the larger flowered ones produce very short lived flowers some of which may only last for one day and then only for a few hours at mid-day.

Notocactus submammulosus and *N. mammulosus*
It is probable that most varieties offered for sale as *N. submammulosus* are in fact *N. mammulosus* the difference being that the true *N. submammulosus* has only one central spine and *N. mammulosus* has two spines.
HABIT: Globular although later becoming cylindrical.

HEIGHT: To 3 or 4 in. (7·6–10·2 cm).

STEMS: Dark or pale green, the ones with paler stems being probably ascribable to *N. submammulosus* with 13–20 low notched ribs.

SPINES: Radials, thin, short greyish becoming yellower near the base. Centrals 1 or 2 as mentioned above, yellowish tipped black, the longest to 0·6 in. (1·5 cm) in length, divergent. Areoles close, at first woolly.

FLOWERS: Produced from the fresh areoles, which if they are going to bear flowers soon make a sort of woolly bud. As with all these sorts of *Notocactus* they are yellow and are formed at the end of a long tube covered in bristles.

Notocactus submammulosus var. *pampeanus* (*N. pampeanus*)

It is still not finally decided whether *N. pampeanus* is a species in its own right, it is certainly a very distinct subspecies if it is a subspecies of the above, but we have seen a few plants which seem to exhibit a continuum of forms between the two species and as far as horticulture is concerned they are exactly identical in their requirements.

HABIT: Globular although later becoming cylindrical.

HEIGHT: To 3 or 4 in. (7·6–10·2 cm).

STEMS: Dark green, depressed at the top with 20 or so broad ribs.

SPINES: Radials up to 10 in number, stout ashen grey forming a fierce protective covering to the plant. Central spine one or two in horticultural specimens, very stiff up to 1·2 in. (3 cm) in length, greyish becoming yellow at the base.

FLOWERS: Yellow produced at the end of a short tube.

Notocactus tabularis (Pl. 22)

HABIT: Globular later becoming cylindrical.

HEIGHT: To 4 in. (10·2 cm).

STEMS: Bluish green with 16 to 20 low notched ribs.

SPINES: Radials 16 to 18 in number up to 1 cm in length, white tipped brown. Centrals up to 4 in number, brown, weak to 1 in. (2·54 cm) in length. Areoles, close, small, with white wool at first.

FLOWERS: Yellow, one of the more difficult varieties on which to obtain flowers when young.

Notocactus concinnus

HABIT: Globular.

HEIGHT: To 4 in. (10·2 cm).

STEMS: Bright green, depressed at the top, with up to 20 low ribs.

SPINES: Radials 10–15, weak, yellow to 0·4 in. (1 cm) in length. Centrals 4 yellow up to 1 in. (2·54 cm) in length. Areoles small, close, at first woolly.

FLOWERS: Yellow, very easy to flower.

Notocactus apricus

HABIT: Globular.

HEIGHT: To 4 in. (10·2 cm).
STEMS: Pale green with 15–20 low slightly tuberculate ribs.
SPINES: Radials 18–20 bristle like, reddish yellow. Centrals four red at the base and yellow nearer the tip. Areoles distant, to 1·57 in. (4 cm) apart, woolly at first.
FLOWERS: Yellow.

Notocactus muricatus
HABIT: Globular, elongating with age.
HEIGHT: To 4 in. (10·2 cm).
STEMS: Pale green with up to 20 low notched ribs.
SPINES: Radials 15–20 weak, spreading, brown. Centrals 3–4 longer and darker than the radials. Areoles borne in the notches on the ribs close up to 0·2 in. (0·5 cm) apart with white wool.
FLOWERS: Yellow.

Notocactus haselbergii (now Brasilicactus haselbergii)
HABIT: Globular occasionally sprouting from the base.
HEIGHT: To 5 in. (12·7 cm) but slow to reach this.
STEMS: Depressed, mid green, with numerous low notched ribs.
SPINES: Radials about 20 in number, very sharp to ½ in. (1·2 cm) in length. Centrals 3–4 yellowish to 1 in. (2·54 cm) in length. Areoles small, up to 0·2 in. (0·50 cm) apart, with white wool.
FLOWERS: Reddish orange.

Notocactus horstii (N. juncineus)
HABIT: Globular but elongating with age.
HEIGHT: To 4 in. (10·2 cm).
STEMS: Pale green, deeply ribbed with up to 12 ribs.
SPINES: Radials 12 or more, weak, bristly, white, occasionally brownish. Centrals usually 4, brown or white. Areoles close, to 5 mm apart.
FLOWERS: Orange somewhat small, produced at the crown of the plant and at first easily confused with *P. gracilis*.

Notocactus scopa
HABIT: Globular when young but soon becoming cylindrical.
HEIGHT: To 5 in. (12·7 cm).
STEMS: Pale green entirely hidden by the soft bristles.
SPINES: Radials numerous, hair-like, snow white. Centrals 3–4 brownish on horticultural specimens somewhat shorter than the type species. Areoles small, close, with a little wool when young.
FLOWERS: Yellow, produced abundantly at the top of the plant.
   There is also a variety *N. scopa* var. *ruberrima* which has crimson red central spines rather than the above rather more brown ones.

Notocactus leninghaussii (Eriocactus leninghaussi)
HABIT: Cylindrical, although very young plants may at first appear globular.
HEIGHT: To 10 in. (25·4 cm).
STEMS: Pale to mid green covered with dense golden hairs with numerous low ribs.
SPINES: Radials 10–15 pale yellow, weak and hair like. Centrals 3–4 in number, up to 1·6 in. (4 cm) in length, deep golden yellow, weak and hair-like. Areoles close with a little white wool when young.
FLOWERS: Normally produced only on plants of 9 in. (22·9 cm) or more in height but very occasionally we have seen plants of 3 or 4 in (7·6–10·2 cm) which have produced flowers.

Care must be taken with this variety to prevent it growing too fast since it can frequently happen that in such circumstances the stem literally explodes and a great gap will appear in the side of the stem. Although the plant will survive this, the gap will never close, and it is probably better to cut off the top and root this. In any case the gap should be dusted with a little sulphur as a precaution against infection.

Notocactus ottonis
HABIT: At first globular but soon elongating and forming offsets at the base.
HEIGHT: To 6 in. (15·2 cm).
STEMS: Mid green with 10–13 broad ribs slightly notched.
SPINES: Few, radials 10–18 short, yellow to brown. Centrals 3–4 on some varieties lacking, slightly longer and stouter than the radials yellowish brown and darker at the tip. Areoles up to 0·6 in. (1·5 cm) apart at first with brownish wool.
FLOWERS: Yellow, abundantly produced and lasting a little longer than most other *Notocacti*.

There are some varieties of this plant now coming onto the market, notably *N. ottonis* var. *linkii* which has almost heart shaped petals and which seems to be slower growing and definitely smaller in general appearance than *N. ottonis*.

Gymnocalycium

The name of this species is derived from two Greek works meaning Naked Calyx, referring to the absence of spines or bristles on the tube from which the flower is produced, they have been replaced by small triangular scales. Some of them are very free flowering and others notably *G. multiflorum* are extremely reluctant to produce flowers. The flowers are produced in a wide variety of colours from the green *G. mihanovichii*, through *G. leeanum* which is rather rare at the moment and has pale yellow flowers to *Gymnocalycium venturianum* which has deep red flowers.

Gymnocalycium damsii (Pl. 13)
The majority of horticultural specimens sold under this name come from a broad spectrum of types between *G. damsii* and *G. mihanovichii*. For the purposes of this work we have regarded anything that is not definitely *G. mihanovichii* and which bears the name *G. damsii*, and conforms to the description below, as *G. damsii*.

HABIT: Small, low globular, producing offsets from the spines at the sides.
HEIGHT: To 3 in. (7·6 cm).
STEMS: Mid green with about 10 low broad ribs. Without lighter horizontal patches and only slightly notched below each Areole.
SPINES: Radials 6–8 up to 0·4 in. (1 cm) in length. Centrals usually absent. Areoles distant up to 0·6 in. (1·5 cm) apart.
FLOWERS: The flower colour varies from a pale green through white to a pale pink on horticultural specimens. The more green there is the greater the affinity with *G. mihanovichii*.

Gymnocalycium mihanovichii
HABIT: Small low, globular, producing offsets from the spines at the sides.
HEIGHT: To 3 in. (7·62 cm).
STEMS: Olive green, occasionally purplish, with 8 broad ribs, more narrow and more deeply notched than in the preceding species with which this should be contrasted, almost invariably with horizontal paler patches between the areoles.
SPINES: Radials 5–6. Centrals absent, greyish yellow, to 0·4 in. (1 cm) in length. Areoles up to 0·4 in. (1 cm) apart.
FLOWERS: Greenish yellow although the outer petals should be flushed red.

In addition to the normal species described above the mutant forms from Japan known as Hibotan are becoming increasingly common. These are normally grown grafted and require considerably more warmth in winter in order to do well. A minimum temperature of 10°C (50°F) is essential if they are to survive. At the moment four distinct colours are known to us, pink, red, yellow and white. The white seems to be the least satisfactory insofar as it reverts to pink after about a year but doubtless some method will soon be found to stabilise it. The red one will produce flowers but they need enormous care to prevent them aborting before opening. (Pl. 42)

Gymnocalycium baldianum venturianum
HABIT: Small, low, globular.
HEIGHT: To 4 in. (10·2 cm).
STEMS: Grey green, occasionally reddish with 10–12 prominently notched ribs.
SPINES: Radials 5, white tipped brown to 1 in. (2·54 cm) in length. Areoles to 1 in. (2·54 cm) apart, slightly woolly.
FLOWERS: Deep purple.

There may be some confusion between this species and *G. venturianum*; however we consider that there are two distinct species of quite different appearance.

G. bruchii (Gymnocalycium lafaldense)
Minor differences between any two plants may be accounted for by the expected results of hybridisation.
HABIT: Low growing, globular, rapidly spreading by offsets to form clumps.
HEIGHT: To 2 in. (5 cm).

44 *Stenocactus lancifer*

45 *Echinocactus grusonii*

46 *Mammillaria microhelia*

47 *Monvillea haagei*

STEMS: Dark green, spiny on top with 12 shallow notched ribs.
SPINES: Radials 12–15, bristly, whitish, brown at the base up to 1 cm in length. Centrals usually absent, occasionally solitary. Areoles very close with a little white felt.
FLOWERS: Pinkish, tinged green on the outside.

Gymnocalycium venturianum (Pl. 12)
HABIT: Globular, usually solitary.
HEIGHT: To 3 in. (7·6 cm).
STEMS: Pale bluish green with nine broad ribs.
SPINES: 5 straw coloured radials, centrals absent. Areoles close up to 1 cm apart.
FLOWERS: Bright red.

Gymnocalycium denudatum (Spider Cactus)
HABIT: Globular.
HEIGHT: To 4 in. (10·2 cm).
STEMS: Deep green with 5–8 broad, blunt ribs.
SPINES: Radials 5–8, yellowish, curved to 1 in. (2·54 cm) in length. Centrals usually absent. Areoles distant to 1 in. (2·54 cm) apart, slightly woolly.
FLOWERS: Green outside, pale green within.

Gymnocalycium gibbosum
HABIT: Globular, becoming more elongated with age.
HEIGHT: To 9 in. (22·8 cm).
STEMS: Bluish green with 12–14 notched ribs.
SPINES: Radials 7–12, spreading to 1 in. (2·54 cm) long. Centrals usually absent. Areoles to 1 in. (2·54 cm) apart with greyish wool.
FLOWERS: White or pale pink.

Gymnocalycium multiflorum
HABIT: Solitary globular.
HEIGHT: To 4 in. (10·2 cm).
STEMS: Dark green with 10–15 broad ribs with narrow furrows between.
SPINES: Radials 7–10, sharp spreading, straw coloured, slightly reddish at the base to 1·2 in. (3 cm) in length.
FLOWERS: Green outside, pale pink within.
   In spite of its Latin name we have not found this species particularly floriferous and it appears that like *G. saglione* it has to be fairly old before it starts producing flowers.

Gymnocalycium saglione (Pl. 6)
HABIT: Globular, usually solitary.
HEIGHT: To 1 ft (30·5 cm) but taking a little while to achieve this size. Most specimens

offered for sale are up to 3 in. (7·6 cm) in height.

STEMS: Greyish green with 10–30 broad ribs, depending on age.

SPINES: Radials, red occasionally black, 8–12 in number, spreading. Centrals 3 slightly arched, the same colour to 1·2–1·6 in. (3–4 cm) in length. Areoles distant, especially in older plants, to 2 in. (5 cm) apart, slightly woolly.

FLOWERS: Produced only on older plants, pink or white.

Gymnocalycium quehlianum (Pl. 11)

HABIT: Low, globular, usually looking as though someone had sat on it.

HEIGHT: To 4 in. (10·2 cm).

STEMS: Bluish green with 8–13 broad ribs.

SPINES: Radials about 5 in number, white or yellowish to 0·4 in. (1 cm) long. Centrals absent. Areoles close, to 1 cm apart, with a little grey wool.

FLOWERS: Large white with a red throat.

This species is subject to a curious disease in winter which causes large sections of the plant to turn reddish brown. We have not been able to ascertain the cause of this but it is definitely not a fungal infection nor is it invariably red spider. It may be connected with temperature but we are not inclined to believe this. At any rate plants which are affected, although unlikely to flower the next year can still recover and will flower the year after although the brown patches may not disappear.

Neoporteria villosa

HABIT: Globular, elongating with age.

HEIGHT: Up to 6 in. (15·2 cm) in height.

STEMS: Greyish green, becoming almost black with age with 13 or more ribs.

SPINES: Radials, 12–16 yellow tipped black, weak, bristly. Centrals up to four in number, thicker up to 1·2 in. (3 cm) in length. Areoles close to 0·4 in. (1 cm) apart with white wool at first.

FLOWERS: A shy flowerer when young, pink or red with a white throat.

Neoporteria subgibbosa

HABIT: Globular, becoming slightly cylindrical with age.

HEIGHT: To 6 in. (15·2 cm).

STEMS: Olive green with 14–16 ribs.

SPINES: Radials dense and numerous, at first yellow, becoming greyer with age. Centrals 4, the same colour.

FLOWERS: Pink.

Echinocactus ingens

HABIT: At first globular becoming cylindrical with age.

HEIGHT: A slow grower eventually up to 5 ft (1·5 m) in height.

STEM: Mid green with up to 8 ribs when young, developing more with age.

SPINES: Radials 8 brownish, Centrals usually solitary. Areoles distance, two 0·6 in.

(1·5 cm) apart with a little yellow wool.
FLOWERS: Produced only on older plants, yellow.

Echinocactus grusonii (Golden Barrel) (Pl. 45)
HABIT: Globular, usually solitary but occasionally we have seen plants forming offsets.
HEIGHT: When old to 4 ft 6 in. (1·4 m) but not normally attaining this height when cultivated in pots.
STEMS: Light green with up to 25 prominent ribs, older plants develop a certain amount of wool on top.
SPINES: Radials stout, straw yellow becoming white with age, 8–10 in number. Centrals 3–5 in number arching downwards.
FLOWERS: Seldom if ever produced on cultivated specimens; yellow.

Astrophytum

These are some of the most ornamental and distinctive Cacti. A *myriostigma* is probably the best one to begin with since it flowers easily and has no spines to speak of. Care should be taken when purchasing *A. ornatum* since nearly all the plants sold under this name are hybrids and lack the distinctive horizontal banding. *A. asterias*, although rewarding in flower and unusual in appearance, is difficult to cultivate on its own roots and is best grown grafted. Some collectors go to considerable lengths to obtain plants of *Astrophytum myriostigma* with an unusual number of ribs, those with 4 ribs have even been given the name of var. *quadricostatum* but we have noticed that when a batch is raised from seed, among 1,000 plants at least 100 have more or less than five ribs and we believe there is really little scarcity value or anything else of note in connexion with these forms.

Astrophytum myriostigma
HABIT: Globular at first becoming cylindrical and erect with age.
HEIGHT: To 4 or 5 in. (10·2–12·7 cm) although slow growing.
STEM: Green completely covered in the true species with white mealy dots, giving it the appearance of being grey. Some varieties have been seen in cultivation with completely green stems and with mealy dots only on the edges of the ribs which are usually five in number.
SPINES: Inconspicuous, to all purposes absent; Areoles distant, brownish.
FLOWERS: Yellow produced on 3 year old plants with the new areoles.

Astrophytum ornatum (Pl. 43)
HABIT: Cylindrical.
HEIGHT: To 1 ft (30·5 cm).
STEMS: Dark green with 5 or more prominent ribs with horizontal bands of white mealy dots in between.
SPINES: 5–11 normally all radials, straight, yellowish becoming brown with age.

Areoles about 0·6 in. (1·5 cm) apart with a little wool in them at first.

FLOWERS: The true species only flowers when about 5 years old but many of the hybrids sold in the shops as *A. ornatum* will flower when younger. Yellow.

Not to be confused with *Astrophytum capricorne aureum* (Pl. 4).

Astrophytum asterias
HABIT: Low, globular.
HEIGHT: Seldom exceeding two inches when grown on its own roots.
STEMS: Dull olive green with 8 broad ribs.
SPINES: Usually absent. Areoles small, white, woolly borne on the edges of the ribs.
FLOWERS: Yellow, fairly freely produced when grafted but otherwise requiring some care.

Ferocactus
These plants are normally distinguished by their vicious spines which are stout, sharp and normally hooked. Where they grow wild they are a great pest since the small ones can easily become lodged in the hooves of horses and can be extremely painful. There is considerable difference between imported and home grown specimens, particularly in relation to the size and colour of the spines. They are slow to flower and must be of considerable age, however their spines are occasionally very beautiful in colour and they grow fairly fast.

Ferocactus latispinus (F. corniger)
HABIT: Globular, solitary.
HEIGHT: In cultivation to 1 ft (30·5 cm).
STEMS: Greyish green with 8 or more ribs when young increasing with age. The ribs are very prominent and conspicuously notched.
SPINES: Radials 6–12 ringed white or red to 1 in. (2·54 cm) long. Centrals 4, vicious, bright red when young to 1·4 in. (3·5 cm) long and hooked. Areoles large, distant with short grey felt.
FLOWERS: Mauve, produced only on well established plants.

Ferocactus viridescens
HABIT: Globular, solitary.
HEIGHT: To 1 ft (30·5 cm) in cultivation.
STEMS: Dark, glossy green, with 13 or more broad ribs.
SPINES: Very variable in number, normally more than nine, at first red becoming russet with age. Centrals 4 as the previous species.
FLOWERS: Green, produced only on old plants.

Ferocactus wislizenii
HABIT: Globular later becoming cylindrical.
HEIGHT: To 2 ft (61 cm).

STEMS: Dark green becoming greyer with age with 15 or more ribs.
SPINES: Radials 15 or more, white, up to 2 in. (5 cm) long. Centrals 4, at first yellowish becoming redder and browner with age.
FLOWERS: Orange or green produced on old plants.

Hamatocactus setispinus
HABIT: Globular at first becoming cylindrical with age.
HEIGHT: Normally up to 2 ft (61 cm) in cultivation.
STEMS: Dark green with 13 conspicuous ribs, although horticultural specimens exhibit considerable variety of form.
SPINES: Radials 12 at first red becoming yellow with age. Centrals 3 hooked. Areoles distant about 0·4 in. (1 cm) apart with short whitish felt.
FLOWERS: Yellow, produced even on seedlings less than 1 year old.

This is a very popular species and there are a large number of forms available in shops and from specialist nurserymen. The most important other species is probably *Hamatocactus hamatacanthus* which has 4 central spines the longest of which is flattened on top. Although most works of reference specify that both *H. setispinus* and *H. hamatacanthus* have a red throat we have seen many plants which are clearly one or the other without this red throat.

Stenocactus (Echinofossulocactus)
This genus is easily distinguished from all others by the presence of numerous deeply divided wavy ridges on which the areoles are born. The botanical name was *Echinofossulocactus* referring to the similarity in appearance between the surface of this species and a badly ploughed field.

Stenocactus zacatecasensis
HABIT: Globular, low.
HEIGHT: To 1 foot, very slow growing.
STEMS: Characteristically divided into numerous wavy ribs. Pale green.
SPINES: Radials variable in number, 8–12, white, short. Centrals 3, brownish longer. Areoles small at first with a little white wool.
FLOWERS: White tipped pink, produced freely on 4 year old plants.

Stenocactus lancifer (Pl. 44)
HABIT: Globular, low.
HEIGHT: To 1 ft (30·5 cm).
STEMS: Mid green, divided into numerous wavy ribs.
SPINES: Variable in number, normally about 8, grey. Areoles distant.
FLOWERS: Large, pink.

Stenocactus hastatus
HABIT: Globular, low.

HEIGHT: To 1 ft (30·5 cm).
STEMS: Pale green, with 30 or more wavy ribs.
SPINES: Radials 5–6, yellowish, Centrals solitary up to 1·6 in. (4 cm) in length.
Areoles distant.
FLOWERS: Pale yellow.

Echinomastus macdowellii
HABIT: Globular, elongating with age.
HEIGHT: To 6 in. (15·2 cm) in cultivation, rather slow growing.
STEMS: Pale green but almost completely obscured by the weak bristly radial spines,
with 20 or more ribs.
SPINES: Radials 15–20 transparent white up to 1 in. (2·54 cm) in length. Centrals 3–4
straw coloured at first becoming white with age up to 6 cm in length. Areoles close
to 0·2 in. (5 mm) apart.
FLOWERS: Pink. Although reputed to be fairly easy to flower even when young we
have found that flowering size is normally only reached after about 6 years.

Sub-tribe E CORYPHANTHANAE

This tribe includes one of the largest families of cacti, the Mammillarias and all
its members are characterised by having tubercles completely surrounding the
stem rather than being borne on ribs. They are also distinguished from other
families in the way their flowers are produced since they appear from in
between the tubercles rather than from amongst the spines. Most Mammillarias
may be induced to flower with no difficulty at all but Thelocacti and Cory-
phanthas are rather more reluctant.

Coryphantha pallida
HABIT: Low, globular forming clumps.
HEIGHT: To 1 ft (30·5 cm).
STEMS: Bluish green with thick tubercles.
SPINES: Radials, 20, white. Centrals usually solitary when young but increasing in
number with age, the lower one curved and tipped black.
FLOWERS: Greenish yellow, large.

Coryphantha radians
HABIT: Globular, elongating with age.
HEIGHT: To 1 ft (30·5 cm).
STEMS: Mid-green with wool in between the tubercles when young.
SPINES: Radials variable in number, normally about 15, yellowish, tipped brown.
Centrals absent. Younger areoles with a little wool in them.
FLOWERS: Yellowish.

Coryphantha clava
HABIT: Cylindrical elongating quickly.
HEIGHT: To 1 ft 6 in. (45·7 cm).
STEMS: Grey green with a little wool between the tubercles at the top of the plant.
SPINES: Radials 9–10, yellow. Centrals up to 4 in number, at first brown but yellowing with age. Areoles woolly at first.
FLOWERS: Yellowish.

Thelocactus bicolor
HABIT: Globular sometimes elongating with age.
HEIGHT: To 1 ft (30·5 cm), but slow growing.
STEMS: Bluish green, the tubercles arranged in 8 rows.
SPINES: Spreading. Radials 10 or more, yellow at the tip, white in the centre and red at the base. Centrals 4 the same colour. Areoles woolly when young.
FLOWERS: Deep red, but produced only on older plants.
There is also a well known variety var. *tricolor* with more red on the spines.

Mammillaria

A very large genus whose members bear a strong resemblance to one another superficially but who have strong individual characteristics. The flowers are generally speaking small and are produced from the axils of the younger tubercles, emerging through the spines. They are on the whole easy to flower, although you should not wait until buds appear before giving any water. As the new tubercles unfold from the centre red spots will appear in the axils and given light and water these red spots will develop into rings of flowers. Probably one of the easiest to flower is *Mammillaria zeilmanniana* which produces rings of bright pink flowers in the spring, however it is extremely susceptible to fungal infections which often wreak their havoc before they are seen, and which is almost impossible to control once seen. Another good variety for the beginner is *Mammillaria rhodantha* frequently sold as *M. bogotensis* which flowers later in the year. The hardier, early flowering varieties include *M. schelhasei* which has greenish yellow flowers and *M. heyderi*, one of the most attractive species with large white flowers. *M. plumosa* is unusual and pretty but difficult and rare, while *Mammillaria bocasana* has attractive seed pods and is a reliable flowerer but tends to rot off in the spring or autumn.

As far as general culture of Mammillarias is concerned we recommend that in the long run it will pay in terms of flower production to put them to rest slightly later and to start them slightly earlier than other varieties. Most of them will always produce flowers and the larger they are and the more offsets they produce the more flowers will be formed as a consequence. It is most important however to inspect the plants twice or three times a week for signs of rotting off. This is best done by knocking the plants out of the pot to see if the root tips are white or brown. If they are brown there is probably something wrong and the most sensible thing to do is to isolate the plant and to dry it out. We have found that an airing cupboard is probably the best method if no radiators are available. If the plant is important it would also be a good idea to remove any offsets which might have formed since at least these will be saved even if the main plant dies, similarly any seed pods.

The only satisfactory method of controlling this damping off is well sterilised soil backed up by hygienic cultivation. If possible two fungicides can be used with some effect—Benlate and Sclex—but for maximum efficiency they must be used together and we do not know whether they are obtainable for amateurs.

The most susceptible varieties are—*M. zeilmanniana, M. bocasana, M. camptotricha, M. decipiens* and *M. elongata. M. schiedeana* and *M. pluomsa* can also present problems even if grafted unless a minimum of 8°C (46°F) can be maintained.

For identification purposes we have followed the generally accepted principle of putting those plants with a watery sap first and segregating to the second half of our list those with a milky sap and a greyish tinge to the stem. When piercing the plants in order to identify them, however, take care to pierce the actual stem and not the tubercles, because certain of the plants in the second half of the list have a milky sap in the stem but not in the tubercles.

SECTION I Hydrochylus K. Sch. (Plants with a watery sap)

Mammillaria elongata
HABIT: Forming clusters, cylindrical.
HEIGHT: To 6 in. (15·2 cm).
STEMS: Much branching, erect or semi prostrate. Cylindrical, bright green with little or no wool in the axils.
SPINES: Radials about 18 in number, usually yellow, occasionally reddish or brown in certain varieties forming a star. Centrals up to four in number but usually absent. Areoles round and losing their wool with age.
FLOWERS: In the true species yellowish but many horticultural varieties have pink flowers probably as the result of hybridisation.

There are several varieties of this, the most commonly seen of which is var. *rufro crocea* where the spines are conspicuously tinted brown and where the stems are almost invariably prostrate.

Mammillaria microhelia (Pl. 46)
This is sometimes referred to as a variety of the preceding species and frequently includes plants of *M. microheliopsis* when sold under the former name.
HABIT: Differs from *M. elongata* in having a solitary stem.
HEIGHT: To 4 in. (10·2 cm).
STEMS: Bright green with a little wool occasionally in the younger axils.
SPINES: Arranged as the name suggests to form a little sun (Greek: *micros* = small; *helios* = sun). Radials very numerous, small but very firm. Centrals usually one but occasionally more. Reddish brown.
FLOWERS: Creamy yellow.

M. microheliopsis differs from this species in being small and having purplish red flowers, but not all plants sold with the purple flowers should be ascribed to *M. microheliopsis*, the most important distinguishing feature of which is probably the pale grey or pinkish tinge on the central spines.

Mammillaria schiedeana
HABIT: Clustering, small globular bodies doing best when grafted.
HEIGHT: To 3 or 4 in. (7·6–10·2 cm).
STEMS: Very dark green with narrow tubercles about 5 mm tall.
SPINES: Weak and hair like. Radials numerous up to 30 in number white at the top and yellow at the base. Centrals usually absent.
FLOWERS: Whitish green appearing amongst the tubercles even on quite young plants.

This species is best grown grafted as offsets do not seem to produce very adequate root systems, but if grafted care should be taken to ensure that sufficient warmth is maintained as otherwise infection can set in round the graft.

Mammillaria plumosa
HABIT: Globular, forming clusters, not dissimilar to the preceding species but white rather than yellowish.
HEIGHT: To 6 in. (15 cm) high, but slow growing, tending to spread rather than grow tall.
STEMS: Dark green, completely obscured by the white feathery spines.
SPINES: Radials numerous, very short arranged like feathers, grey to white. Areoles close, round, with much white wool.
FLOWERS: Small, white, with black seeds.
A very popular but still somewhat rare species.

Mammillaria prolifera
HABIT: Low, spreading rapidly forming clumps.
HEIGHT: To 6 in. (15 cm).
STEMS: Dark green, almost completely obscured by the spines.
SPINES: Radials numerous, hair-like and white, differing from *M. plumosa* in having ordinary spines rather than feathered ones. Centrals to 10 in number although usually about 5, at first straw coloured but later becoming white. Areoles slightly woolly at first.
FLOWERS: Greenish yellow, just showing through the spines.
There are several varieties of this, none of them differing significantly from the species, the most commonly seen of which is probably var. *texana*.

Mammillaria decipiens
HABIT: Low, spreading rapidly, forming clumps.
HEIGHT: To 4 in. (10·2 cm).

STEMS: Globular, deep or pale green with narrow soft conical tubercles to $1\frac{1}{2}$ in. (3·8 cm) long and $\frac{1}{4}$ in. (6 mm) thick with a few bristles between.
SPINES: Radials, 7–9, needle like, white occasionally tinged brown. Central solitary, brown to 1 in. (2·54 cm) in length.
FLOWERS: White, occasionally tinged pink, hard to see amongst the tubercles.

Mammillaria camptotricha
  This species could be confused with the preceding one but differs in having longer, yellow and more twisted central spines.
HABIT: Low, spreading, clustering and forming clumps.
HEIGHT: To 4 or 5 in. (10·2–12·7 cm).
STEMS: Deep green with slender cylindrical tubercles to $2\frac{1}{2}$ cm long, with bristles in the axils.
SPINES: Radials, 4–8 bristle-like, yellowish and twisted up with one another, tending to obscure the stem. Areole small and hairless.
FLOWERS: White, tinged green on the outside, appearing between the tubercles.

Mammillaria schelhasei
HABIT: Clustering, globular.
HEIGHT: To 6 in. (15 cm).
STEMS: Grey green, with cylindrical but slightly angled tubercles which are easily detached, somewhat woolly in the axils.
SPINES: Radials about 15, straight, white and bristle-like to 0·4 in. (1 cm) long. Centrals, brownish to 0·6 in. (1·5 cm) long the longest of them hooked. Areoles small and woolly.
FLOWERS: Greenish, occasionally tinged pink.

Mammillaria zeilmanniana (Pl. 20)
HABIT: Freely clustering, branching both from the base and from the sides of the stem.
HEIGHT: To 6 in. (15 cm), but seldom achieving this.
STEMS: Dark green, glossy when young with oval tubercles.
SPINES: Radials 15–18, white, hair-like and soft. Central 4, reddish brown strongly hooked and catching easily in one's clothing. Areoles woolly when young but bare when old.
FLOWERS: Pink.
  There is also a white form of this *M. zeilmanniana alba* which appears to be slightly hardier and just as floriferous. (Pl. 19)

Mammillaria bocasana
HABIT: Low, forming clumps, branching mainly from the base.
HEIGHT: To 6 in. (15 cm).
STEMS: Bluish green, with slender cylindrical tubercles to 0·4 in. (1 cm) long with fine

white hair in the axils.
SPINES: Numerous, hair-like radials and 1–4 centrals the longest of which is hooked.
Areoles round with wool when young.
FLOWERS: White, occasionally tinged pink. Fruit produced a year after pollination, long and a brilliant fluorescent pink.

Mammillaria kunzeana
HABIT: Spreading and low, forming clusters.
HEIGHT: To 4 in. (10·2 cm).
STEMS: Glossy green with cylindrical tubercles, with bristles between.
SPINES: Radials 25 or more about 0·4 in. (1 cm) long, white, thin. Centrals 4 grey or straw coloured, occasionally dark brown, at least one hooked. Areoles with a little wool when young.
FLOWERS: Yellow, tinged pink.

Mammillaria erythrosperma
HABIT: Forming clusters, spreading.
HEIGHT: To 4 in. (10·2 cm).
STEMS: Dark green, globular, with cylindrical tubercles and a few bristles in between.
SPINES: Radials, about 18 in number, straight, white, slender, to 0·4 in. (1 cm) in length arranged like a star. Centrals 1–3 yellowish.
FLOWERS: Deep red.

Mammillaria aurihamata (Pl. 14)
HABIT: At first globular but elongating with age, forming offsets from the base and sides.
HEIGHT: To 6 in. (15 cm).
STEMS: Dark glossy green with cylindrical tubercles and a few curly bristles in between.
SPINES: Radials about 20, pale yellow or straw coloured. Centrals, 4, thicker, at first pale yellow but deepening in colour with age, hooked. Areoles with a little wool.
FLOWERS: Pale yellow.

Mammillaria wildii
HABIT: Clustering. Globular at first becoming cylindrical with age.
HEIGHT: To 6 in. (10·2 cm).
STEMS: Bluish green with cylindrical tubercles, and a few hairs in the axils.
SPINES: Radials, 8–10, white or rose, bristly to 5 mm long. Centrals 3–4 stouter, longer, yellow, the uppermost hooked. Areoles at first woolly.
FLOWERS: The true species has white flowers but horticultural specimens may have pink ones due to hybridisation.
    This is one of the best cacti to grow indoors as it is quite tolerant of a little more warmth during the resting period which will not inhibit it from flowering.

Mammillaria pygmaea
HABIT: Elongated, club shaped, forming clusters.
HEIGHT: To 4 in. (10·2 cm).
STEMS: Glossy bluish green.
SPINES: Radials about 15 in number, white. Centrals 4, yellowish, the lower ones slightly hooked.
FLOWERS: Red, produced on quite small plants.

Mammillaria bombycina
HABIT: Globular, eventually forming clusters but relatively slow to produce offsets at first.
HEIGHT: To 8 in. (20·3 cm).
STEMS: Bright green with flat cylindrical tubercles to 0·6 in. (1·5 cm) in length, with dense wool in between.
SPINES: Radials up to 40 in number, white, spreading, bristly. Centrals four, frequently tinged red, hooked.
FLOWERS: Red, produced normally only after the third or fourth year.

Mammillaria spinosissima
HABIT: Very variable, solitary, cylindrical.
HEIGHT: To 8 in. (20·3 cm) although attaining greater heights in the wild.
STEMS: Mid green with conical tubercles. Axils with a little wool, especially when young.
SPINES: About 25 radials, bristle-like, of very variable length, white or straw coloured. Centrals 7–10 varying in colour from white to brown. Areoles at first with a little wool.
FLOWERS: Produced only on older plants, bright red.

Mammillaria bogotensis (M. columbiana var. bogotensis)
HABIT: Solitary, globular at first becoming club shaped with age.
HEIGHT: To 6 in. (15 cm).
STEMS: Mid green becoming greyer with age. Axils very woolly when young.
SPINES: Radials about 25, white occasionally straw coloured. Centrals 1–6, usually the latter, brown when young but becoming paler and more straw coloured with age. Areoles with white wool at first which later becomes brown.
FLOWERS: Reddish, produced amongst the woolly axils at the top of the plant.

Mammillaria rhodantha (Pl. 17)
HABIT: Extremely variable, but generally solitary, becoming elongated with age although at first globular.
HEIGHT: To 8 in. (20·3 cm).
STEMS: Greyish green, sometimes darker, axils with more or less wool.
SPINES: 16–20 radials, mainly white, sometimes yellow. Centrals 3–6 yellow, red or

brown, often darker at the tip. Areoles with a little wool.
FLOWERS: Red or pink produced in a ring round the top.

Mammillaria mundtii
One supplier we have seen is marketing this as *M. nundtii* and the amateur buying labelled varieties and seeking them in these pages should be advised at this point to allow for such spelling mistakes when looking up something he has bought.
HABIT: Globular.
HEIGHT: To 6 in. (15 cm).
STEMS: Dark green, woolly at the top when older.
SPINES: Radials 10, thin, white. Centrals 2, straight, spreading, brown. Areoles with white wool when young.
FLOWERS: Red, produced above the tubercles.

Mammillaria kewensis
Many horticultural specimens sold under this name belong properly to *M. hidaloensis* with which it is very similar, the main distinction being that *M. kewensis* has pinker spines and paler flowers.
HABIT: Solitary, cylindrical.
HEIGHT: To 1 ft (30·5 cm).
STEMS: Dark green with a little white wool in the younger axils.
SPINES: Radials generally absent, if present normally indicating more affinity with *M. hidalgensis*. Centrals about 4, spreading slightly, purplish. Areoles at first woolly but later bare.
FLOWERS: Pale pink.

SECTION II Galactochylus (Plants with a milky sap)

Mammillaria celsiana
HABIT: Solitary, forming clumps only when older. Globular at first becoming club shaped with age.
HEIGHT: To 8 in. (20·3 cm).
STEMS: Greyish green with much white wool produced between the tubercles.
SPINES: Radials about 25, thin, white to 0·3 in. (7 mm) long. Centrals usually 4 but sometimes more, dark yellow tipped brown. Areoles small and woolly.
FLOWERS: Pink, produced amongst the thick wool at the top.

Mammillaria klissingiana
HABIT: Globular at first, becoming cylindrical with age.
HEIGHT: To 6 in. (15 cm).
STEMS: Glossy green completely obscured by the spines with much wool between the tubercles.
SPINES: Radials 30 or more, very thin and bristle-like, white. Centrals 2–4, white

tipped strongly with red when young. Areoles with white wool when young.
FLOWERS: Brilliant carmine.

M. lanata is frequently offered for sale but most specimens belong properly to
M. klissingiana. The true *M. lanata* is much woollier and lacks central spines. It is
still somewhat uncommon in cultivation.

Mammillaria parkinsonii
HABIT: Globular becoming club shaped with age, at first solitary but later forming
clusters.
HEIGHT: To 6 in. (15 cm).
STEMS: Grey green almost completely obscured by the spines with wool and bristles
between the tubercules.
SPINES: Radials 25, bristle-like, white. Centrals 2, white with brown tips.
FLOWERS: Yellowish, often hidden amongst the wool.

Mammillaria hahniana (Pl. 16)
HABIT: Globular, very hairy; branching only when older.
HEIGHT: To 8 in. (20·3 cm).
STEMS: Mid green, completely obscured by masses of long white hairs. Axils pro-
ducing many long white bristles.
SPINES: Radials about 30 in number, white, thin. Centrals 2, white or transparent
tipped brown.
FLOWERS: Red, freely produced even in quite young plants but requiring full
sunshine.

Mammillaria heyderi (Pl. 15)
One of the finest species of *Mammillaria* and regrettably still not generally available.
It is quick to grow and easy to flower. We have even seen some specimens flower
twice in the same year.
HABIT: Low, hemispherical, becoming elongated in its fifth or sixth year.
HEIGHT: To 4 in. (10·2 cm).
STEMS: Pale or grey green, usually unbranched, with a little wool in the younger
axils.
SPINES: Radials 20, white, with brown points. Centrals usually solitary, reddish brown
with an almost black tip.
FLOWERS: White tinged green extruding through the spines between the tubercles.

Mammillaria magnimamma (M. centricirrha)
An extremely variable species. The plants sold under this name by most growers
include many plants approximating to *M. compressa* and even to *M. collinsii.* A very
general description is offered here. Plants with very hairy axils probably should
belong under *M. nejapensis* which has yellowish flowers or under *M. collinsii.*
HABIT: Clustering with globular stems.

HEIGHT: To 8 in. (20·3 cm).
STEMS: Dark to grey green with conical tubercles and woolly axils.
SPINES: Very variable in number and length. Normally about 4 and grey in colour.
FLOWERS: Red, produced among the white wool, on older plants.

Mammillaria gigantea
HABIT: Solitary, globular.
HEIGHT: To 4 in. (10·2 cm).
STEMS: Greyish green with white wool in the axils and numerous tubercles which distinguishes it from the preceding species.
SPINES: Radials 12, white, very short. Centrals much longer up to 1·2 in. (3 cm) in length, curving downwards, yellowish brown when young but becoming grey with age.
FLOWERS: Greenish yellow, produced on older plants.

Mammillaria uncinata (Pl. 18)
HABIT: Globular, depressed on top.
HEIGHT: To 2·4 or 2·8 in. (6 or 7 cm).
STEMS: Globular with lizard-shaped flattened dark green tubercles about 0·4 in. (1 cm) high with wool between when older.
SPINES: Radials 2·4A3·2 in. (6–8 cm) white, the uppermost very prominent, brown, 0·4 in. (1 cm) in length. Centrals solitary, hooked, about 0·6 in. (1·5 cm) in length. At first dark brown becoming paler with age.
FLOWERS: Cream coloured, produced at each tubercle.

Mammillaria compressa
HABIT: Very variable, but forming clumps, globular, flattened.
HEIGHT: To 4 in. (10·2 cm).
STEMS: Mid green with a white wool in the upper axils, the tubercles packed close together.
SPINES: 4–7, sometimes lacking altogether, of variable length, white becoming grey with age.
FLOWERS: Red, produced only on older plants and then sparingly.

Sub-tribe F EPIPHYLLANAE

Both this and the next tribe are epiphytic in the wild, that is to say they grow on trees. Although the *Epiphyllums* which characterise this particular tribe are not particularly demanding in their requirements. On the whole they appreciate a little more shade in summer, although we have frequently found it very satisfactory to put them out as soon as the new growth has been made in order to harden it during the summer. In this way we have obtained two crops of flowers on some plants. The plants should, however, be placed in a cool situation in the garden, the emphasis being mainly on good air circulation, and they should be brought in before the beginning of September.

Zygocactus truncatus (Christmas Cactus)
HABIT: Hanging with branching jointed stems.
STEMS: From $1\frac{1}{2}$–$3\frac{1}{2}$ in. (3·8–9 cm) in length, flat with toothed edges and a flattened apex.
SPINES: More bristly than spiny, produced from the flattened ends.
FLOWERS: In the true species deep red.

There are many varieties of this plant which is very popular, they vary from the pale orange *Weihnachtsfreude* to the fluorescent pink *Margrit Koeniger*, however, unless buying from a specialist grower it is seldom possible to obtain accurately named hybrids. There is also a white flowered one which is somewhat rare.

Schlumbergera gaertneri (Whitsun Cactus)
HABIT: Bushy, branching freely, more erect than the previous species.
STEMS: Oval, up to 4 in. (10·2 cm) in length, notched on the margins, mainly flattened but occasionally three angled.
SPINES: 1–2, bristly, weak, produced in the areoles at the notches. The joints are cut off at the growing tip.
FLOWERS: Scarlet red, produced on the terminal branches at the cut off end.

Much hybridisation has been carried out with this species and a number of attractive hybrids between it and *Rhipsalidopsis* are now available in many shades. We have also seen a very pale pink one which may have some *Zygocactus* sap in it. (Pl. 30)

Epiphyllum
Although there are only about 17 species in this genus there are innumerable hybrids, a full discussion on which would be outside the scope of this book. In general the plants are very large and therefore it is usually not possible for the beginner with limited space at his disposal to have large numbers of them. We can recommend from our own experience *E.* × *elegantissimum* which seems to need less staking than many, and *E.* × *cooperi*, which although large is unusual on account of its white flowers which spring up from the base of the stems.

Propagation is best done by means of stem cuttings which should be taken at the widest point on the 'leaf' (in fact the stem) so as to provide the maximum rooting surface.

The description given below is deliberately somewhat general so as to include as much as possible.
HABIT: Bushy, occasionally hanging.
HEIGHT: To 3 or 4 ft (91 cm–1·2 m) but normally requiring staking.
STEMS: Leaf like, with wavy, notched edges.
SPINES: Normally present round the narrower stems especially in *E.* × *cooperi* and *E.* × *ackermannii*, only present in the notches in the stem when young, otherwise

more bristle-like than spine-like. Areoles small, hidden in the notches.
FLOWERS: Red, orange, pink or white, generally, a true yellow has yet to be found.

Nopalxochia phyllanthoides var. *Deutsche kaiserin*
This species is often sold as an *Epiphyllum* but differs in having more bell shaped, less open, flowers which are invariably pink.
HABIT: Shrubby branching very freely.
HEIGHT: To 3 or 4 ft (91 cm–1·2 m).
STEMS: Flat, spear shaped, pale green, often tinged with red.
SPINES: Usually absent.
FLOWERS: Pink, bell shaped, produced very freely over a long period.

Sub-tribe G RHIPSALIDANAE
Differs from the previous sub-tribe in being generally much smaller in size, and in having angled stems. The exception to this are plants of the subgenus *Phyllorhipsalis*, with flattened stems, the most commonly sold of which is *Rhipsalis houlletiana*. Not recommended for beginners as they generally require more warmth and more shade than most other cacti. However the varieties listed below will do reasonably well along with other cacti if given slightly more shade even though it is not possible to preserve a sufficiently moist atmosphere.

Culture is in general similar to that for Epiphyllums but care should be taken to water them occasionally in winter, especially *Rhipsalidopsis rosea* which should not be allowed to dry out.

Rhipsalidopsis rosea (Pl. 29)
HABIT: Short low shrub, later hanging, branching freely.
STEMS: Sometimes flat, occasionally angled, often both kinds on the same plant, oval, normally green, but occasionally with a strong purple tinge.
SPINES: Bristly rather than spine-like, produced in the areoles.
FLOWERS: Produced in the late spring from the long areole at the tip of the terminal stems. Pale purple, very pretty. As mentioned earlier several hybrids between this and *Schlumbergera gaertneri* are now available and are well worth trying. (Pl. 30)

Hariota salicornioides (Hatiora salicornioides) (Drunkard's Dream)
This plant derives its somewhat surprising English name from the bottle like shape of its stems!
HABIT: Bushy, upright or hanging.
STEMS: Of 2 kinds, one long and slender bearing a cluster of terminal branches at the end. Generally cylindrical to bottle shaped, in circles.
SPINES: Short, white, bristly.
FLOWERS: Produced in areoles on the terminal stems, small, yellowish green.

Rhipsalis houlletiana

HABIT: Hanging, branching freely.

STEMS: Of 2 kinds, one cylindrical, the other flat. Pale to greyish green with very wavy notched edges, up to eight inches long.

SPINES: Absent. Areoles with a little wool.

FLOWERS: White, produced from the margins of the stems.

Rhipsalis paradoxa

HABIT: Hanging, branching into two periodically at the tips.

STEMS: Generally 3-angled, short, pale green, often tinged red.

SPINES: Bristly, only present on the younger areoles which are slightly woolly.

FLOWERS: Only produced on fairly well established plants at the tips of the joints, white.

13

A general list of succulents, with descriptions

For this list we propose to assemble the species in alphabetical order since as far as the amateur is concerned we feel this will be as satisfactory as the botanical order. The list is slightly more limited in scope than that for the cacti since there are in many cases such slight differences between the species that enough will be learned from a study of the more representative species within each genus.

Adromishus cooperi
HABIT: Small—eventually forming clumps.
HEIGHT: Short and compact.
STEMS: Upright, succulent.
LEAVES: Very thick and fleshy, glaucous green, flecked with reddish brown rounded at the edges and narrowing towards the base.

Aeonium arboreum atropurpureum
HABIT: Slender, graceful, upright with a long stem.
HEIGHT: Cultivated specimens are generally small and seldom exceed 2 ft (61 cm).
STEMS: Slender, about ½ in. (1·3 cm) thick, becoming brown with age as the older leaves fall off.
LEAVES: Produced in a rosette at the top of the plant, dark purple, occasionally with a greenish band at the edges. Outer leaves up to four inches long, falling off with age.
FLOWERS: Only produced on fairly old plants, yellow.
NOTE: *Aeoniums* usually die off after flowering and so it is advisable to save the seed. Apart from this and some other species many of them grow to considerable size and look very ungainly; they are consequently not recommended for the amateur.

Aloe variegata (Partridge Breasted Aloe)
HABIT: Low growing, compact, forming clumps with age.
HEIGHT: Seldom exceeding 9 in. (23 cm) when not in flower.

STEMS: Almost completely obscured by the triangular heavily keeled leaves; more easily seen at the base of the plant.

LEAVES: Triangular, very thick and fleshy. Mid-green flecked regularly with white, giving it its name.

FLOWERS: Produced on plants 3 years old or more, regularly from the base of the leaves. The red flowers are produced on the end of a long stem.

NOTE: It is a common mistake with this plant to give it too much sunlight. In fact it needs less sunlight than most other succulents and will do better in a living room off the windowsill than in full sunlight. Care should also be taken when watering not to allow the water to collect at the base of the leaves since this can cause the plant to rot off.

Aloe aristata

HABIT: Low, forming clumps.

HEIGHT: About 4–5 in. (10·2–12·7 cm) when not in flower.

STEMS: Stemless.

LEAVES: Erect, forming a dense rosette. Obtusely triangular in section and fleshy with a thread-like tip. The surface of the leaves is covered with white warts and the edge has small white spines on.

FLOWERS: Reddish orange, borne on a stem up to 16 in. (40·6 cm) long on plants of three years of age.

NOTE: This plant is readily propagated from offsets and is definitely best kept underpotted.

Aloe ferox

HABIT: Upright with a short stem.

HEIGHT: In the wild up to 12 ft (3·65 m) but rarely attaining this in cultivation.

STEMS: In cultivated species circular, up to $\frac{3}{4}$ in. (1·9 cm) in diameter.

LEAVES: Thick fleshy, well armed with spines on all sides.

FLOWERS: Flowers are very rarely produced on cultivated specimens.

NOTE: *Aloe concinna* is sometimes sold as *A. ferox* but should be distinguished by the white markings on the leaves and its more visible stem. The leaves are less dense and bent back at the tips.

Aloe arborescens

HABIT: Upright, rambling, often trained up walls to great advantage.

HEIGHT: Up to 12 ft (3·65 m).

STEMS: Bare on older plants, sometimes developing aerial roots.

LEAVES: In the wild up to 2 ft (61 cm) long but rarely reaching this size on cultivated specimens, grey-green with waved spiny edges.

FLOWERS: Only produced on very old plants.

Anacampseros rufescens
HABIT: Short, erect or sprawling when older.
HEIGHT: Up to 3 in. (7·6 cm) tall.
STEMS: Hardly visible between the dense leaves, branching with age.
LEAVES: Reddish purple arranged in dense pyramidal spiral round the stems normally with white hairs about ½ in. (1·3 cm) long.
FLOWERS: Produced on plants once they are about 3 in. (7·6 cm) high but needing very strong light to encourage them to open. Photographic lamps are ideal for this purpose, but even so the pale pink petals will rarely open evenly.

Argyroderma octophyllum
HABIT: At first easily confused with the pebble plants or *Lithops*, small pebble-like.
HEIGHT: Rarely greater than 1 in. (2·54 cm) although an older clump may build itself up more than this.
STEMS: None.
LEAVES: Glaucous green, 2–4, almost spherical in shape and in its native habitat of Namaqualand difficult to distinguish from the surrounding pebbles.
FLOWERS: Freely produced up to ¾ in. (1·9 cm) across, yellow.

Argyroderma testiculare
This is generally similar to the above although in fact most plants sold as *A. testiculare* are more likely to be *A. octopetalum*. The type *A. testiculare* has white flowers.

Bergeranthus multiceps
HABIT: Forming dense clumps, stemless.
HEIGHT: Up to 2 in. (5 cm) high.
STEMS: None.
LEAVES: Erect or sprawling to 2 in. (5 cm) in length, triangular in section light green in colour.
FLOWERS: Fairly freely produced in moderate sunlight, yellow inside and red outside up to 1 in. (2·54 cm) in diameter.

Bergeranthus scapiger has bluish green leaves which are much longer and golden yellow flowers. *Bergeranthus vespertinus* is distinguished by its dark spots on the upper leaf surfaces.

Ceropegia woodii
HABIT: Trailing or climbing.
HEIGHT: Up to 12 ft (3·65 m).
STEMS: Long, very slender, purple, individual branches sometimes up to a yard long. Corms are produced at intervals at the nodes.
LEAVES: Flat, heart-shaped, grey, attractively marbled with purple.
FLOWERS: Fairly freely produced, like small candles upright and tubular with very

dark purple petals.

This species may be easily propagated by removing the tubers or corms which form at the nodes and by rooting them in a propagator in a moist atmosphere. It has also been used as grafting stock for other members of the same family — *Asclepiada-ceae*— for example *Hoodias*.

Conophytum minutum
HABIT: Pebble-like, although more upright and elongated than *Argyrodermas*, forming clumps even when fairly young.
HEIGHT: Up to ¾ in. (1·9 cm) in height.
STEMS: Negligible, normally an extension of the rootstock rather than a true stem.
LEAVES: Grey-green, flattened on top, similar in appearance to a Lithops.
FLOWERS: Purple, fairly freely produced.

Conophytum albescens
HABIT: As the preceding species.
HEIGHT: Up to 1 inch.
STEMS: As above.
LEAVES: Two, slightly triangular in section, greyish tinged with red at the edges and densely covered with short white down.
FLOWERS: Yellow; freely produced about 1 in. (2·54 cm) in diameter.

Other species of *Conophytum* worth trying are *Conophytum bilobum* which requires some heat in the winter and some moisture since it starts to flower in May and rests during March and April, and *Conophytum obcordellum* which has fragrant flowers and has grey-green leaves with dark dots. During the resting period the outer skin of *Conophytums* dies off as the nourishment is transferred to the fresh young plant growing below it. The beginner should therefore not assume that they have died!

Cotyledon undulata
HABIT: Upright, and slender.
HEIGHT: To 1 ft (30·5 cm).
STEMS: Slender, grey-green, densely covered with mealy down.
LEAVES: Produced opposite one another at regular intervals up the stem. Semi-circular in shape, grey-green in colour with wavy edges and a white wax covering which disappears when wetted.
FLOWERS: Produced at the end of the stems, orange to red.
NOTE: This species is slightly delicate and if spraying takes place with Malathion care should be taken to prevent it coming into contact with this species which will otherwise suffer.

Crassula arborescens
HABIT: Bushlike, forming a stout stem and in appearance like a miniature tree.
HEIGHT: To 3 ft (91 cm).
STEMS: Thick and succulent. Becoming trunk-like and brown in older plants.

LEAVES: Grey, oval, narrowed at the base produced opposite one another. Plants with darker leaves are normally *Crassula portulacea*, which has much smaller leaves seldom exceeding 1 in. (2·54 cm) in width. Both these are frequently sold under either name and there are several hybrids between them.

FLOWERS: Produced only on older plants, produced from the ends of the older shoots when grown in cool well lit positions. Generally white although *C. arborescens* is occasionally tinged pink. The quantity of flowers is variable, large numbers being produced one year and only a few the next. It seems advisable to allow the fresh shoots to ripen by standing the plants outside if possible during the summer.

Crassula falcata (Rochea falcata)
HABIT: Upright.
HEIGHT: To 3 ft (91 cm).
STEMS: Slender to ¾ in. (1·9 cm) thick, firm with short intervals between the leaves.
LEAVES: Very thick, grey green and fleshy, completely surrounding the stem at the base and normally twisted. On well developed plants they can be over 4 in. (10·2 cm) in length.
FLOWERS: Produced on plants of 2 years of age in a large terminal cluster. Brilliant red and frequently owing to their number requiring a stake for the flower stem in order to keep it upright.
NOTE: If the leaves are removed from the plant and inserted into potting compost they will form a cluster of young plants at the base. Before potting up this cluster should be divided carefully in order to encourage the plant to develop its characteristic large leaves.

Crassula lycopodoides
HABIT: Upright or sprawling, much branched, like a small heather.
HEIGHT: In cultivation seldom more than 6 in. (15 cm) high.
STEMS: Completely obscured by the dense covering of tiny leaves.
LEAVES: Very small, arranged in 4 rows round the stem giving it a square appearance. Dark green, somewhat triangular in shape.
FLOWERS: Insignificant, yellow, appearing in the leaf axils and looking like a fine powder.
   There are several varieties of this species including a monstrose one, but by far the most attractive is the variegated *C. lycopodoides variegata*.

Crassula perforata
HABIT: Erect at first but later sprawling.
HEIGHT: Up to 1 ft (30·5 cm).
STEMS: Slender, seldom branching unless the growing tip is damaged, grey.
LEAVES: Opposite and as its name implies perfoliate, that is to say the stem appears to grow from between the 2 leaves which seem joined together round it. Grey-green, frequently with a reddish margin. At first triangular, becoming more oval in shape.

FLOWERS: Insignificant, produced at the tips.

This is another species which does not care for most horticultural insecticides which will spoil its greyish coating. It also appreciates considerable sunlight since it will tend otherwise to grow very long and leggy.

Crassula schmidtii
HABIT: Dwarf, compact and clump forming.
HEIGHT: Seldom exceeding 4 in. (10·2 cm).
STEMS: Slender, occasionally trailing in older plants, normally well concealed by the thin tapering leaves.
LEAVES: Slender, tapering, occasionally dotted with red, mid-green.
FLOWERS: Pink produced in terminal clusters for the greater part of the year.

After flowering has finished the shoots of this species seem to suffer a severe setback and form branches from the base. Consequently after several years one can be left with a very unattractive looking specimen. Cuttings may be rooted in a propagating frame and this is best done in peat although we have had some difficulty in persuading them to root. However it does repay the effort as by potting them up into a pot each year a fresh compact plant can be maintained.

Crassula socialis
HABIT: Low growing forming a ground cover.
HEIGHT: Seldom exceeding 1 in. (2·54 cm).
STEMS: Insignificant, completely obscured by the leaves.
LEAVES: Broadly triangular, produced in four rows round the stem, pale green.
FLOWERS: Small, white, produced freely even on quite young plants, on the end of long flower stems rising from the centre of the rosettes.

Cyanotis somaliensis
HABIT: Trailing or climbing.
HEIGHT: Seldom greater than 6 or 7 in. (15–17·8 cm) in cultivation.
STEMS: Slender, trailing unless supported, mid green.
LEAVES: Keeled at the base, dark green, clasping the stem about 2½ in. (6·3 cm) long. The under sides and edges of the leaves have grey hairs growing from them.
FLOWERS: Blue, produced in clusters amongst the leaves at the tip of each shoot.

This species can grow very poorly and tend to sprawl with long gaps between the leaves unless pruned rigorously by pinching out the tips at intervals in order to force it to branch. The pinched-out tips may then be re-rooted if required in the same pot or another, in order to maintain a bushy base for the plant.

Echeveria
Echeverias may be dealt with under two headings, those forming low growing rosettes such as *Echeveria derenbergii* and those forming small shrubs on longer stems, the most commonly seen of which is *Echeveria gibbiflora*.

Echeveria derenbergii
HABIT: Low growing forming rosettes.
HEIGHT: Seldom exceeding 2 in. (5 cm).
STEMS: Non-existent when young.
LEAVES: Fleshy, rounded at the top and ending in a small red point, pale green with a red margin.
FLOWERS: Borne on a short stem at the side of the rosette, reddish yellow.

Echeveria carnicolor
HABIT: Low growing forming rosettes.
HEIGHT: Seldom exceeding 2 in. (5 cm).
STEMS: Normally stemless but a small stem may develop if potted too deeply in the pot.
LEAVES: Less rounded at the edges than *E. derenbergii* with a broader point. Rosette more open. The leaves are pinkish with a slight silvery touch.
FLOWERS: Borne on short stems at the side, reddish orange.

Echeveria gibbiflora
HABIT: Shrubby.
HEIGHT: Up to 2 ft (61 cm).
STEMS: Up to ½ in. (1·3 cm) thick, branching, frequently needing support.
LEAVES: Glaucous grey-green, long, up to 10 in. (25·4 cm), rounded at the tips and gently narrowing towards the stem. Borne in rosettes at the ends of the branches.
FLOWERS: Produced profusely at Christmas time from the sides of the rosettes on long stems. Reddish orange.
 There are many varieties of *E. gibbiflora*, the more commonly seen of which are *E. gibbiflora metallica*, whose leaves have a distinct metallic sheen and are more rounded than long; the plant is also generally smaller: also *E. gibbiflora carunculata* which has growths on the surface of the leaves.

Echeveria glauca
HABIT: Low growing forming rosettes spreading by runners.
HEIGHT: Seldom exceeding 2 in. (5 cm).
STEMS: Normally absent except for runners.
LEAVES: Forming an open rosette, greyish with a red edge, almost round.
FLOWERS: Borne on slender stems, reddish outside and yellow within.

Echeveria leucotricha
HABIT: Forming a small shrub.
HEIGHT: Up to 1 ft (60·5 cm).
STEMS: Short, lightly covered with white hairs.
LEAVES: Boat shaped densely covered with white hairs up to 3½ in. (8·9 cm) long, tinged brown towards the point.

FLOWERS: Borne on stems at the sides of the rosettes, bright red.

Echeveria multicaulis
HABIT: Forming a small shrub.
HEIGHT: Low, up to 1 ft (30·5 cm).
STEMS: Becoming woody with age, branching, bearing a loose rosette of leaves at the tips.
LEAVES: Fresh green becoming browner near the tips and narrowed towards the base.
FLOWERS: Red outside, yellow within, borne on branches.

Echeveria nodulosa
HABIT: Small and shrubby.
HEIGHT: Up to 2 ft (61 cm).
STEMS: Thin, branching freely.
LEAVES: Dull bluish-green with a reddish marking down the centre and along the edges.
FLOWERS: Red outside, brownish-yellow within.

Echeveria pulvinata (Chenile Plant)
HABIT: Resembling *E. leucotricha* whose description should also be consulted if in doubt.
HEIGHT: Up to 1 ft (30·5 cm).
STEMS: Short and lightly covered with white felting.
LEAVES: Similarly covered with white hairs, cultivar Ruby edged with red. Distinguished from *E. leucotricha* by being much broader and flatter.
FLOWERS: Produced on long stems, reddish.

Echeveria setosa
HABIT: Stemless, forming dense rosettes.
HEIGHT: Up to 3 in. (7·6 cm).
STEMS: Absent.
LEAVES: Dark green tipped with red and covered with white hairs.
FLOWERS: Produced on stems rising from the rosettes through spring and summer, red and yellow.

Echidnopsis cereiformis
HABIT: Upright, columnar, branching.
HEIGHT: To 1 ft (30·5 cm).
STEMS: Very succulent somewhat like a cactus but spineless. Ribs flattish, 10 or more with tubercles.
LEAVES: Rudimentary or absent.
FLOWERS: Star shaped with 5 petals, yellow, produced at the tips of the stems.

Euphorbia caput-medusae (Medusa's Head)

HABIT: Low, sprawling.

HEIGHT: Seldom exceeding 1 in. (2·54 cm) although growing tips may at first point upwards.

STEMS: Trailing branches, variable in length, and a small spherical main-stem usually completely obscured by the branches.

LEAVES: Produced at the growing tips, mid green, very small.

FLOWERS: Yellow, produced only on older plants.

There is also a cristate variety of this *E. caput-medusae cristata* which is particularly attractive in its own right. However, it is worth noting that the normal branches which this form produces make excellent specimens of the normal type and are generally more vigorous than the true specimens.

Euphorbia grandicornis

HABIT: Upright, columnar, deeply ribbed, branching.

HEIGHT: In the wild up to 30 ft (9·1 m) but relatively slow growing in cultivation.

STEMS: Deeply ribbed and divided into segments often corresponding to yearly growth but occasionally representing more. The segments are generally 3 to 4 ribbed and have wavy edges.

LEAVES: Rudimentary on the growing tips of the plants. Spines large, giving the plant a very ferocious appearance, up to 2 in. (5 cm) long.

FLOWERS: Small yellow, on very short stems, produced from the edges of the segments between the spines.

Euphorbia hermentiana (E. trigona)

Considerable confusion exists between the botanical *E. hermentiana* and the botanical *E. trigona*. In practice we have found that nearly all plants sold as *E. hermentiana* by nurserymen both in England and Europe are in fact *E. trigona*. Conversely we have frequently seen plants labelled for sale as *E. trigona* which are in fact *E. hermentiana*. The description below is based upon cultivated material which we have seen for sale as *E. trigona*.

HABIT: Upright, columnar, ribbed sharply, branching.

HEIGHT: As *E. grandicornis* but slightly faster growing and branching more freely.

STEMS: Fairly slender, frequently needing staking. Dark green frequently becoming woody below, and tending to discolour at the joints with other branches when too old.

LEAVES: Very small (as distinct from the true *E. trigona* which has fairly well developed leaves), soon falling. Spines fairly short, seldom more than 5 mm in length.

FLOWERS: Inconspicuous, yellow, produced only on older plants between the spines on the edges of the ribs.

Euphorbia ingens

HABIT: Upright, columnar, ribbed, branching.

133

HEIGHT: To 30 ft (9·1 m) in the wild but growing slowly in cultivation.
STEMS: 4 to 5 angled, slightly waved at the edges of the ribs becoming woody with age.
LEAVES: Inconspicuous, produced only at the growing tip. Spines stiff, short and close to 0·4 in. (1 cm) in length.
FLOWERS: Produced only on older specimens.

Euphorbia mammillaris (Corncob Cactus)
HABIT: Upright, columnar with horizontal branches.
HEIGHT: To 2 ft (61 cm) but generally requiring staking.
STEMS: Olive green, cylindrical to 1·4 in. (0·35 cm) thick, with 8–17 ribs with tubercles, giving the plant its English name. Branches very thin where they join the main stem, much thicker at the growing tip.
LEAVES: Rudimentary, soon giving way to occasional stiff buff spines.
FLOWERS: Produced on twig-like stems, small, yellow.

Euphorbia meloformis
HABIT: Spherical.
HEIGHT: 3 to 4 in. (7·6–10·2 cm).
STEMS: Globular with 8–10 deep ribs the sides of which have pale red lateral stripes
LEAVES: Rudimentary, produced only at the growing point and not persisting.
FLOWERS: Produced fairly freely on the ends of twig like branches which persist and become woody spines. The actual flowers are very small and yellow.

Euphorbia millii (E. splendens prostrata) (Crown of Thorns)
HABIT: Shrubby, may become sprawling with age.
HEIGHT: To 4 ft (1·22 m).
STEMS: Stiff and branching, green at the tips and purplish-brown below. Heavily armed with small spines to ½ in. (1·3 cm) long, the variety *E. millii* 'Aalbaeumle' raised by H. Koeniger of Aalen has flexible spines which are not so vicious as the more typical ones.
LEAVES: Small, rounded at the tips and narrowing towards the base. Dull green and easily dislodged. Most varieties tend to shed large numbers of leaves when moved
FLOWERS: Red, borne normally in pairs on the ends of branches up to 3 inches long rising above the leaf joints off the stems.

E. millii var. *splendens*
Within the description below are included plants of the variety most commonly seen—*E. splendens* var. 'Bojeri'.
HABIT: Bushy and shrubby.
HEIGHT: To 5 ft or more if trained up a trellis.
STEMS: Slightly furrowed, branching, grey below and green at the growing tips.
LEAVES: Larger than in *E. millii* up to 2 in. (5 cm) long broad at the tip and narrowing

towards the main stem.

FLOWERS: Red, larger than in E. *millii* up to $\frac{1}{2}$ in. (1·3 cm) in diameter, produced on sticky, forked stems.

There is also a variety on the market E. *splendens* 'Tananarive' also raised by H. Koeniger which has much larger leaves and yellow flowers.

Euphorbia obesa

HABIT: Small, spherical.

DIAMETER: To 6 in. (15 cm).

STEM: Globular and spineless with 8 broad vertical ribs, mainly purplish although sometimes greener near the growing point at the centre.

LEAVES: Normally absent, when present extremely rudimentary.

FLOWERS: Very small produced as in E. *meloformis* from the centre.

E. *obesa* is distinguished from E. *meloformis* mainly by its intense purple colour and its more globular appearance. E. *meloformis* has much deeper ribs.

Euphorbia resinifera

HABIT: Upright, columnar, branching.

HEIGHT: To several ft.

STEM: 4 angled, grey-green with small brown spines on the edges.

LEAVES: Very rudimentary, small and brown.

FLOWERS: Only produced on very mature plants.

E. *resinifera* makes a very attractive little plant although it is at first easily mistaken for a true cactus. Although it branches freely it makes slow growth.

Euphorbia submammillaris

HABIT: Dwarf shrub, much branching.

HEIGHT: To 7 in. (17·8 cm).

STEMS: Club-shaped about $\frac{3}{4}$ in. (1·9 cm) thick branching vertically off the main stems and each other, eventually forming a dense mounded cushion.

LEAVES: Fairly rudimentary and soon falling. Produced at the growing tip.

FLOWERS: Borne on short forked branches near the growing tips, yellow; the short twig-like stems harden after the flowers fall and become spines.

Euphorbia trigona (E. hermentiana)

HABIT: Upright, columnar, angled and branching.

HEIGHT: To several feet, faster growing than E. *hermentiana*.

STEMS: 3, angled with fairly clear variegation down the centre as opposed to E. *hermentiana* which has only slight variegation if at all.

LEAVES: Freely produced and very conspicuous as opposed to E. *trigona* whose leaves are very small.

FLOWERS: Inconspicuous, yellow, produced only on older plants.

Euphorbia valida
HABIT: Small, globular.
HEIGHT: To 3 in. (7·6 cm).
STEMS: Globular with 8–10 broad ribs. Deep olive green.
LEAVES: Very rudimentary, small and green.
FLOWERS: Produced as in *E. obesa* and *E. meloformis* from twig-like branches at the centre of the plant.

It is probable that *E. valida* is in fact a hybrid between *E. obesa* and *E. meloformis* certainly we have seen plants for sale under this name exhibiting a wide range of characteristics between these two varieties.

Faucaria tigrina (Tiger's Jaw, Tiger's Chaps)
HABIT: Short forming rosettes on a short stem.
HEIGHT: To 4 or 5 in. (10·2–12·7 cm).
STEMS: Very short.
LEAVES: Very succulent, broadly triangular in section with flexible teeth at the edges giving the plant its English name. Grey-green in colour, often with a slight tinge of red if grown in full sunlight.
FLOWERS: Large, yellow, daisy-like.

Faucaria tuberculosa
HABIT: Short, forming rosettes.
HEIGHT: To 4 or 5 in. (10·2–12·7 cm).
STEMS: Very short.
LEAVES: As the former species but darker green and with fewer teeth; with white warts on the upper surfaces.
FLOWERS: Yellow as in the preceding species.

Haworthia cuspidata
HABIT: Stemless forming rosettes, suckering from the base.
HEIGHT: To 3 in. (7·6 cm).
STEMS: Absent.
LEAVES: Very succulent, keeled and furrowed above, often with glassy patches at the tips. Pale green.
FLOWERS: White, borne on long stems on older plants.

Haworthia reinwardtii
HABIT: Small, erect, branching from the base.
HEIGHT: To 6 in. (15 cm).
STEMS: Upright, completely obscured by the leaves.
LEAVES: Short, claw-shaped and covered with white spots. Slightly purplish green completely covering the stem.
FLOWERS: Borne on long stems from the side of the main stem, white.

Haworthia papillosa
HABIT: Rosette forming, short.
HEIGHT: To 2 in. (5 cm).
STEMS: Virtually stemless.
LEAVES: Up to 1½ in. (3·8 cm) long, narrow, covered with large white tubercles.
FLOWERS: White, borne on long stems.

Hoya carnosa
HABIT: Climbing.
HEIGHT: To several ft.
STEMS: Thin, woody, with long internodes.
LEAVES: Leathery, dark green, elliptical, produced opposite one another on the stem.
FLOWERS: White to pale pink, produced in clusters from the axils of the leaves or from last year's growth, scented.

Hoya carnosa can be difficult to flower when grown in a pot, we recommend that it be planted in the greenhouse if possible and trained up a wall. When grown in a pot the best results are probably obtained if it is trained round a hoop so that the air can get at all parts of the stem equally. *H. carnosa* is not so commonly seen as the variety *H. carnosa variegata* which very seldom flowers but produces attractive cream, green and occasionally red variegated leaves.

Kalanchoe beharensis
HABIT: Upright, shrubby, occasionally branching.
HEIGHT: To several ft but fairly slow growing.
STEM: About ½ in. (1·3 cm) thick, green, covered with grey hairs.
LEAVES: Broadly triangular in shape and up to 8 in. (20·3 cm) long. At first covered densely with grey and rust coloured hairs but later only with grey ones.
FLOWERS: Very seldom produced in cultivation.

K. beharensis is extremely worthwhile and although the plants become unattractive in later life when the lower leaves fall, it is a simple matter to strike the top part of the stem as a cutting.

Kalanchoe blossfeldiana
Most of the varieties exhibited for sale are hybrids of *Kalanchoe blossfeldiana* and other *Kalanchoe* species. The true species has red flowers but all shades from red through orange and pink to yellow may be obtained.
HABIT: Dwarf shrubby, often appearing to form clumps.
HEIGHT: Depending on variety, some quite dwarf, others up to 2 ft (61 cm).
STEM: Thick, green, often obscured by the leaves especially on the dwarf varieties.
LEAVES: Oval with wavy edges, dark green, occasionally purplish. Produced opposite one another on short stalks.
FLOWERS: Produced at the ends of the stems and often also on branches rising from the axils of the upper leaves. Of various colours in a branched cluster.

Kalanchoe daigremontiana (Mother of Thousands)
HABIT: Upright, slender, often requiring staking, especially if grown with insufficient light.
HEIGHT: Normally up to 3 ft (91 cm), although it may be more if the light is poor.
STEM: Thin, to $\frac{2}{3}$in. (1·6 cm) thick, mottled with purple and later becoming woody.
LEAVES: Triangular, green mottled with purple, to 8 in. (20·3 cm) long. Distinguished by the presence of little plantlets growing round the edges.
FLOWERS: Produced on the ends of the stems, reddish.

This is one of the most popular and most easily grown plants. It is extremely tolerant and if anything goes wrong with your main plant it is a very simple matter to root the little plantlets growing round the edges of the leaves, many of which will probably fall off and root themselves in the pot in any case.

Kalanchoe fedtschenkoi marginata
This is becoming quite scarce now but is worth obtaining if plants can be found.
HABIT: Dwarf, shrubby, branching.
HEIGHT: To 1 ft 6 in. (45·7 cm).
STEM: Thin, purple, green when young.
LEAVES: Oval, normally purple although becoming more green in winter, variegated with cream and red. Occasional shoots may be produced which are completely white. These are best removed since no further growth will take place at such points.
FLOWERS: This plant is a shy flowerer and will normally only produce blooms if harshly treated over the winter. Even when they do appear it is quite difficult to get them to open. The flowers are yellowish green and bell-shaped and are produced in a spike from the ends of the stem.

Kalanchoe tubiflora
HABIT: Upright, slender, often requiring staking.
HEIGHT: To 3 ft (91 cm).
STEM: Slender, green, often mottled with greyish-purple spots.
LEAVES: Tubular in shape, green mottled with greyish-purple, producing young plantlets at the end of the leaves rather than on the edges.
FLOWERS: Produced at the ends of the stems, reddish orange.

Kleinia articulata (see *Senecio articulatus* var. *globosus*) (p. 142).

Lampranthus aureus
HABIT: Erect or spreading.
HEIGHT: When erect to 1 ft 6 in. (45·7 cm).
STEMS: Very slender and tough when young, green, becoming brown with age.
LEAVES: Green, triangular in section, up to 2 in. (5 cm) long, normally with a very slight frosting, smooth.
FLOWERS: Large, yellow, daisy-like, up to 2 in. in diameter but only produced with considerable sunshine.

Lithops
The detailed identification of *Lithops* would take one beyond the scope of this particular work; a general description is given below followed by notes on some of the more common varieties.
HABIT: Dwarf forming clumps.
HEIGHT: Seldom exceeding 2 in. (5 cm).
STEMS: Rudimentary and normally indistinguishable from the tap root.
LEAVES: Normally 2, occasionally 4. Opposite, semi-circular, very succulent. The two opposite leaves giving the appearance of a pebble. Normally mottled and of varying colours from grey to green.
FLOWERS: Produced from the crack between the leaves in the centre, large, daisy-like in a variety of hues.
   Lithops bella is brownish-yellow in colour, to 1 in. (2·54 cm) high with a rounded top and white flowers.
   Lithops comptonii is olive green with yellow flowers.
   Lithops erniana is reddish green with white flowers.
   Lithops fulleri is a very small one with a rounded top and grey leaves with brown markings; flowers—white.
   Lithops karasmontana grey to brown leaves with white flowers.
   Lithops lesliei flat topped, leaves brown with green grooves, flowers yellow.
   Lithops marthae rounded top, grey leaves often lined or dotted. Flowers yellow.
   Lithops mickbergensis leaves reddish grey and grooved, flowers white.
   Lithops olivacea olive green leaves with a deep groove and yellow flowers.
   Lithops pseudotruncatella leaves with a shallow groove, flowers yellow.
   Lithops umdausensis leaves olive green with a deep fissure, flower white.

Oliveranthus elegans (now Echeveria harmsii)
HABIT: Erect and shrubby.
HEIGHT: To 2 ft (61 cm).
STEMS: At first green becoming woody with age.
LEAVES: Mid green, up to 1½ in. (3·8 cm) long pointed at the tips and narrowing towards the stem, produced in great profusion giving the plant the appearance of a miniature tree.
FLOWERS: Red outside, yellow within, produced on side shoots off the main stem.
   Oliveranthus elegans makes an excellent houseplant, it is easy to flower and propagation is relatively easy either by seeds or by cuttings. It is a fairly fast grower and needs more feeding than most other succulents.

Orostachys spinosus
HABIT: Clump forming, stemless.
HEIGHT: To ¾ in. (1·9 cm).
STEMS: Absent.
LEAVES: Of two different kinds, the smaller central ones close, set triangular in

shape, the outer ones arranged more loosely and more elliptical in shape with a conspicuous pointed tip.

FLOWERS: Seldom produced when cultivated indoors.

Pachyphytum amethystinum

HABIT: At first forming rosettes later sprawling on long stems.

STEMS: Branching, up to $\frac{1}{2}$ in. (1·3 cm) thick, grey tinged purplish.

LEAVES: Broadly pointed at the tip, narrowing towards the base, grey tinged purple like the stems; falling normally in their third year leaving the stems looking unattractive and sprawling.

FLOWERS: Bright red.

Pleiospilos bolusii

HABIT: Short, forming clumps with 2 thick leaves.

HEIGHT: Up to 2 in. (5 cm) in height.

STEMS: Absent.

LEAVES: Thick, brownish green, stone like, broadly triangular in section up to 2 in. (5 cm) in length, flecked with dark green dots.

FLOWERS: Yellow, daisy-like, produced between the central pairs of leaves.

Rhombophyllum nellii (Elkhorns)

HABIT: Normally forming clumps on the ground but occasionally developing a short stem.

HEIGHT: To 2 in. (5 cm).

STEMS: Usually absent, when present completely obscured by the leaves.

LEAVES: Thick, narrowly triangular in section. Broad at the tip, club-shaped, usually lobed giving the plant its appearance of Elk's horns. Pale bluish-grey with small darker dots.

FLOWERS: Produced very freely especially on plants raised from seeds. Sometimes 2, normally 1 borne on a stalk, yellow, daisy-like, up to $\frac{3}{4}$ in. (1·9 cm) in diameter.

Rhombophyllum rhomboideum

HABIT: Stemless, forming clumps.

HEIGHT: To 2 in. (5 cm).

STEMS: Absent.

LEAVES: Much flatter and more broadly triangular in section than the preceding species. They are supposed to be lozenge shaped in outline when viewed from the top, but this may be hard to see in cultivated specimens. However, they lack the twin lobes of the previous species and are greyish-green covered with whitish dots. Some varieties have white teeth on the edges.

FLOWERS: Up to 1 in. (2·54 cm) in diameter, daisy-like, golden yellow.

Sansevieria trifasciata var. *laurentii* (Mother-in-Law's Tongue)
HABIT: Usually stemless forming clumps.
HEIGHT: Up to 3 ft (91 cm) in cultivation.
STEMS: Absent or completely obscured by the leaves.
LEAVES: Erect, rising from ground level clasping one another. Dark green in the centre with a golden margin. Lance-shaped and sharply pointed at the tip. The true species *S. trifasciata* does not have this variegation and has greyish-green leaves with horizontal bands of darker green. As the clump grows larger the leaves become longer.
FLOWERS: Produced only on harshly treated plants, grey, on a stem produced from the side between the leaves.

This is probably one of the most commonly seen houseplants let alone succulents, it is almost impossible to kill when kept indoors although in a greenhouse it is essential to guard against humidity in winter which can rot off the stems. In order to propagate the variegated variety it is necessary to take suckers from below the soil where they look like tubers and to root these, alternatively you may wait until there are some leaves above ground on the new clump and root this. If a portion of the leaf is cut off horizontally and stuck in the earth in a temperature of 25°C (70–80°F) young green shoots without the golden margin will be produced at the base.

Sedum lineare variegatum
HABIT: At first erect and then semi prostrate with age.
HEIGHT: To 3 in. (7·6 cm).
STEMS: Very thick, usually unbranched unless damaged.
LEAVES: Up to ½ in. (1·3 cm) long, thin, lance-shaped, green with a white margin.
FLOWERS: Star-shaped, yellow.

Sedum morganianum (Burro Tail)
HABIT: Hanging, forming clumps from the base.
LENGTH: To several feet although very slow growing.
STEMS: Thin, hanging, usually unbranched.
LEAVES: Thin, spindle-shaped, pale to yellowish green, clustered very thickly around and completely obscuring the stem giving the plant its common name.
FLOWERS: Produced on the ends of older stems, pale pink, star-shaped.

S. morganianum is a decorative asset in any collection but it is very temperamental and seems to require slightly more warmth than other *Sedums*. It is also intolerant of over-watering and for this reason is often grown in a clump of moss fixed onto a piece of bark. It also seems to prefer a slightly more shaded position in summer as it tends otherwise to dry out too fast.

Sedum pachyphyllum (Jelly Beans)
HABIT: Erect, branching from the base.
HEIGHT: To 1 ft (30·5 cm) then tending to sprawl on the ground unless staked.

STEMS: Thin, grey-green at first, becoming woody with age.

LEAVES: Long, thin cylindrical, grey-green, looking just like jelly beans might be supposed to appear, occasionally tipped red. Very easily detached and normally falling with age leaving the main stem looking very unattractive.

FLOWERS: Star-shaped, bright yellow, produced at the ends of the branches.

Sedum sieboldii var. *medio variegatum*

HABIT: Clump forming, putting up shoots from the base.

HEIGHT: Normally sprawling but younger plants may be up to 6 in. (15 cm) height.

STEMS: Very slender, normally arched, annual, green or occasionally white.

LEAVES: Broadly circular, grey with a white dash in the centre produced in rings at intervals on the stem.

FLOWERS: Pale pink, produced profusely at the ends of the stems.

This plant has annual shoots although the rootstock may persist for several years. Propagation is best done by division or by seed and during the winter when the shoots have died down it is best kept dry and only just above freezing. It should not be considered dead and thrown away.

Sempervivum

These plants are frequently known as houseleeks or 'St Patrick's Cabbage' and are best grown outside in the garden doing well in a sink garden or an old outhouse roof where they are absolutely hardy. Indoors or in a greenhouse they tend to become too leggy. The most frequently seen variety is *S. tectorum* which also grows wild in England and has reddish-purple leaves arranged in rosettes. Less commonly seen but equally worthwhile is *S. arachnoideum* whose leaves are connected by white hairs giving it the appearance of being draped in cobwebs. *Sempervivums* as a whole seem to differ widely in appearance depending upon the soil in which they are grown.

Senecio articulatus var. *globosus (Kleinia articulata)*

HABIT: Branching from the stem, low, shrubby.

HEIGHT: To 1 ft (30·5 cm).

STEMS: Jointed, globular, pale grey-green.

LEAVES: Produced on long arching stems from the tip of the main stems deeply divided into three, the central lobe in turn three lobed and broadly lozenge shaped, darker green than the stems.

FLOWERS: Pale yellow, groundsel-like.

Senecio stapeliaeformis (Kleinia stapeliaeformis)

HABIT: Erect forming tufts from the base.

HEIGHT: To 1 ft (30·5 cm) in cultivation.

STEMS: Thin, upright, angled, pale silver-green with darker vertical lines.

LEAVES: Small awl shaped, dark green, soon withering and falling.

FLOWERS: Red, like a groundsel.

Senecio macroglossus variegatus
HABIT: Climbing, usually unbranched unless pinched or damaged.
HEIGHT: To several ft when trained, otherwise trailing.
STEMS: Very thin, twining around support with long gaps between the leaves.
LEAVES: Broadly triangular, very similar to an ivy with which it is easily confused. Dark green with a creamy margin, occasionally all cream, the fresh leaves at first very small, only becoming larger with age or if the growing tip is pinched out, waxy.
FLOWERS: Yellow, daisy-like, produced from the tips of the stems on older plants, more especially when they are planted out.

This is rapidly assuming an important place among collections since it grows rapidly and is almost indestructible. In order to maintain its attractive appearance it is best to pinch out the growing tips which may be easily rooted. This will encourage the younger leaves to become larger and will make the plant produce the new leaves closer together. Otherwise it tends to produce one leaf every foot and soon becomes an unwelcome weed.

Stapelia grandiflora
HABIT: Erect forming clumps from the base.
HEIGHT: To 1 ft (30·5 cm).
STEMS: Erect, green to 1 ft (30·5 cm) in height, broadly four angled.
LEAVES: Small green, produced at intervals on the angles of the stem giving the appearance of teeth.
FLOWERS: Large, brownish, hairy, of evil appearance and small, to six inches in diameter but produced only on well established plants.

Stapelia variegata
HABIT: Erect, forming clumps from the base.
HEIGHT: To 6 in. (15 cm).
STEMS: Erect, 4 angled, smooth, branching near the base, green mottled with purple.
LEAVES: Produced on the edges of the stems, small dark green.
FLOWERS: Pale yellow with purple spots.

Stapelias are doubtless a curiosity but their revolting smell which is intended to be similar to that of rotting meat means that they are best placed outdoors while in flower so that one's enjoyment of the rest of one's collection is unspoilt.

Tradescantia navicularis
HABIT: Sprawling, only occasionally branching.
HEIGHT: Young plants may occasionally be erect up to 3 in. (7·6 cm) in height.
STEMS: Completely obscured by the leaves, thin, arching.
LEAVES: Produced in 2 ranks, overlapping one another boat-shaped, greyish-green pointed at the tip.
FLOWERS: Freely produced on stems borne from the axils of the leaves, rosy pink with 3 petals.

This hardy little plant is not now as common as it used to be but if carefully tended will bear flowers during winter as well as throughout the summer and is consequently extremely worthwhile.

Yucca
Yuccas are best grown outdoors where they will normally flower after about six years once they become established, although not perfectly hardy they will withstand a normal English winter.

The above is a general guide to some of the more usually seen succulents; there are of course hundreds of others, but we hope that with the aid of the above list you will be able to approximate to the correct family, and once you have correctly named a dozen or so varieties you will find yourself instinctively going for the correct names in order to find another. Below we have attempted to set out a general table of cultivation methods for the different types we have mentioned.

NAME	POSITION	TEMPERATURE	WATERING	PROPAGATION	FLOWERING
Adromischus	Sun	5°–8°C (41°–45°F)	SP,SU,a,w.	L.C.	Summer
Aeonium	Sun	5°–8°C (41°–45°F)	Sp,SU,a,w.	St.C.	Summer when old
Aloe variegata	Shady	5°–8°C (41°–45°F)	SP,SU,A,w.	Offsets	Summer
Other Aloes	Sun	5°–8°C (41°–45°F)	SP,SU,a,w.	Offsets	Summer
Anacampseros	Full sun	8°C (45°F)	SP,SU,A,w.	Seeds	Summer full sun
Argyroderma	Full sun	4°–5°C (41°F)	SU,A,$P̸,W̸.	Seeds	Late autumn
Bergeranthus	Very sunny	4°–5°C (41°F)	sp,S,a,w̸.	Seeds	Mid summer
Ceropegia	Slight shade	8°C (44°F)	SP,SU,a,w.	St.C.	Summer
Conophytum bilobum	Very sunny	8°–10°C (45°–50°F)	$̸P,SU,A,w.	Seeds	Early spring
Others	Very sunny	8°–10°C (45°–50°F)	$̸P,Su,A,w.	Seeds	Late summer
Cotyledon	Sunny	5°C (41°F)	sp,SU,A,w.	St.C.	Late summer
Crassula	Sunny	5°C (41°F)	SP,SU,A,w.	St.C., L.C.	Spring–summer
Cyanotis	Sunny	8°C (44°F)	Sp,SU,A,w.	St.C.	Summer
Echeveria	Sunny	5°–8°C (41°–45°F)	Sp,SU,A,w.	St.C., L.C.	Spring
Echidnopsis	Slight shade	8°C (45°F)	sp,SU,A,w.	St.C.	Summer
Euphorbia	Sun	8°C (45°F)	SP,SU,a,w.	St.C.	Spring–autumn
Faucaria	Very sunny	5°C (41°F)	$̸P,SU,A,W̸.	Seeds	Autumn
Haworthia	Sunny	5°C (41°F)	sp,SU,A,w.	Offsets	Early summer
Hoya	Slight shade	8°C (45°F)	SP,SU,A,w.	St.C.	Summer
Kalanchoe	Sun	10°C (50°F)	SP,SU,A,w.	St.C., L.C.	Summer
Lampranthus	Very sunny	5°C (41°F)	SU,A,$̸P,W̸.	Seeds	Summer–autumn
Lithops	Very sunny	5°C (41°F)	Sp,SU,A,W̸.	Seeds	Autumn
Oliveranthus	Sunny	5°C (41°F)	SP,SU,A,w.	St.C., L.C.	Spring
Orostachys	Sunny	5°C (41°F)	SP,SU,A,w.	Offsets	Summer
Pachyphytum	Sunny	5°C (41°F)	sp,SU,A,w.	St.C., L.C.	Summer
Pleiospilos	Very sunny	5°C (41°F)	$̸P,SU,A,W̸.	Seeds	Autumn
Rhombophyllum	Very sunny	5°C (41°F)	$̸P,SU,A,W̸.	Seeds	Late summer

Sansevieria	Sunny	8°C (45°F)	SP,SU,A,w.	Offsets	Spring
Sedum	Sunny	5°C (41°F)	sp,SU,A,w.	St.C.	Autumn
Sempervivum	Sunny	5°C (41°F)	SP,SU,A,w.	Offsets	Autumn
Senecio	Sunny	8°C (45°F)	SP,SU,A,w.	St.C.	Summer
Stapelia	Slight shade	8°C (45°F)	sp,SU,A,w.	St.C.	Summer
Tradescantia	Sunny	5°C (41°F)	SP,SU,A,w.	St.C.	Late summer
Yucca	Sunny	5°C (41°F)	sp,SU,A,w.	Seeds	Summer

SP,SU,A,W.	Water freely during spring, summer, autumn and winter, i.e. about once or twice a week.
̸SP,̸SU,̸A,̸W.	Do not water at all during these periods.
sp,Su,a,w.	Water only once a month or so during these periods unless there are clear signs of shrivelling.
St.C.	Stem Cuttings.
L.C.	Leaf Cuttings.

14

Ornamental bowls of succulents

Collections of succulents are becoming increasingly popular when planted in bowls and we have consequently decided to include a few notes on their cultivation. When planting up such a bowl for yourself take care not to put the plants too close together. They should have sufficient room for light to penetrate to all parts of all the plants; failure to do this will result in poor growth and even damping off.

Start with excellent drainage at the bottom. This can be either broken up bits of clay pots, coarse shingle, charcoal or any other substance. Although it is essential to have this in a plastic bowl we think it is a good policy to have this drainage even in a clay or stoneware one. This is because the bowls for sale on the market frequently have non-porous glazes on them to prevent moisture seeping through onto the table.

Fill the bowl of your choice with a layer about 1 in. (2·54 cm) deep of this drainage material and then place the plants of your choice in their approximate positions in the bowl. Small cacti are seldom of sufficient interest in themselves to make an attractive bowl, and if a large one is not available you could select an attractively shaped piece of bark, a small rock, or even vine shoots and use this instead. Note that this should take the place of plant, you should not try to put three small cacti *and* a large stone in a bowl that would normally only accommodate three plants. This point is frequently overlooked and often leads to bowls being spoilt. For this reason the authors recommend the planting of boat-shaped or elliptical bowls with cacti rather than the more conventional circular ones.

Having placed your plants and ornamentation carefully, fill in the cracks between them with more cactus compost of the same kind as that in which the small plants are potted. If for any reason you are not certain of the type of soil in plants you have bought we suggest that you free the soil carefully round the outermost roots and then fill in the cracks between the plants with the soil mixture outlined earlier in the book. Do not press the soil in too firmly; it is sufficient if the plants will stand upright in the bowl without toppling about. As soon as they are planted to your satisfaction water the bowl thoroughly and set it in a warm sunny place to get it going. Remember it is just as though the plants have been repotted and great care should be taken with the bowl until it is obvious that the plants like their new container and start to grow. It is best therefore if bowls are planted up in late spring or early summer, as this is when plants are growing at their best. Just after flowering is better than just before and we would under no circumstances recommend planting a cactus that was showing actual buds.

There is to our mind an unfortunate tendency amongst many nurserymen to cover the tops of succulent bowls with coloured pebbles. This is certainly not necessary for the successful cultivation of succulents in bowls and to our mind cannot but detract from the natural beauty of the plants. However, there is an even more unfortunate tendency to cement these coloured pebbles together with glue. This has a definitely deleterious effect on the plants and on the soil structure as neither can breathe properly, and should you unwittingly buy such a bowl we strongly recommend that you remove the coloured stones altogether if they are glued.

Occasionally when bowls have to travel long distances for export or import reasons the surface of the soil round the plants is covered lightly with a sort of clay or plaster to prevent the soil spilling out. It is normal for the distributor to remove this covering before putting the bowl on display, but should you get a bowl in which you cannot see any soil we suggest that you pick off anything covering it up.

As far as types go much will depend on the individual and the purpose for which the bowl is being planted. Generally speaking, it is best not to mix cacti and other succulents in the same bowl as they both require different treatment; also most succulents tend to grow faster than cacti and will tend to swamp the bowl in a short time. If you simply must have something in flower in the bowl and you have no cacti in flower, or in spite of the instructions given in the book are still unable to flower those that you have, then we would recommend *Echeveria harmsii* or *Aloe aristata* as two good varieties which are sufficiently tolerant of adverse conditions to enable them to grow with the cacti. If you do make up such a mixed bowl treat it as you would a cactus bowl, that is to say keep it completely dry during the winter, except in a centrally heated room.

Similarly, if you buy a mixed bowl we would suggest that it is better to remove the succulents or the cacti (whichever it is which you don't want) carefully, taking cuttings if it is not possible to remove them without damage to the root systems of the other plants, and plant them up separately. They will do much better.

After having decided whether you want a cactus bowl or a bowl made up of other succulents, you should consider the mixture carefully. In doing this bear in mind what we have said about numbers and do not overfill the bowl. Within this constraint you should try to provide as great a variety of forms as possible. One upright one, a clustering one and a globular one, e.g. *Cereus peruvianus*, *Chamaecereus silvestrii* and a *Rebutia* would make the smallest size bowl. Larger bowls might include an *Opuntia* (remember these tend to grow rather large) a *Notocactus* (which will flower later on) and one of the *Parodias*. We cannot recommend *Mammillarias* as being particularly suitable for bowl work because of their tendency to damp off and for this to spread to other plants before there is time to do anything about it. If you wish to include a *Mammillaria* we would recommend one of those with large tubercles and thick skin such as *Mammillaria bogotensis* or *Mammillaria heyderi*, at all costs avoid *Mammillaria zeilmanniana*; although initially very attractive this rots off so easily that it can later become a curse.

A bowl of succulents offers considerably more scope but generally speaking most succulents require a larger bowl than cacti since they grow faster. Exceptions would be bowls comprising *Lithops* and other slow growing members of the family. When planning your bowl of succulents give some thought to the chart of growing and resting periods which we set out at the end of the list of succulents because it would be disastrous to mix succulents with different resting periods.

For the larger display we prefer the Continental habit of marshalling the plants like an army division. This tends to emphasise the form rather than to detract from it, especially if most of the plants are small ones. Accordingly if it falls to you to set up a display we strongly suggest that you mass them together in similar varieties or otherwise as similar as possible in order to achieve maximum impact. The occasional really large specimen amongst them will then appear all the more spectacular. But peering around for small plants in tiny pots in an ocean of sand is not conducive to sustained interest amongst the uninitiated!

If arranging a bowl for exhibition, then rules and conventions must of course be ascertained beforehand.

Index

Main entries appear first

Ants 65

Cactaceae, tribes of 72–73, 10
Cacti, colours of the flowers of 12
  drainage 11, 15
  drips 24
  grafting 62
  general culture 18–24
  heating 22
  in the house 19
  natural location of 19
  recommended species of 30–44, 13
  selection of 30–44
  situation 9, 30
  staking 24
  transplanting 49–51
  uses of fruits of 12–14
  ventilation 23, 11
  watering 19–22
Compost, definition of 15–17
  John Innes 16
  leaf-mould 16
  production of 15
  seed 17
  selection of 16
  succulent 17, 25
  Cuttings 58–61

Diseases 64–71
  fungal 70–1

Grafting 62
Greenhouses, cacti 18

Heating 22, 55

Insect pests 64–69

John Innes potting composts 16, 25

Liquid manures 16

Mealy bug 65–66

Pests 64–69
Propagating frames 61
Propagation of succulents 52–7, 58–63, 144–5

Red Spider 66
Resting months 144–5, 11, 20

Scale insects 66
Seed 52–57
  composts 17, 54
  failure of 55
  heating 55
  sowing 52–57
  transplanting 55–6
  watering 54–5
Staking 24, 27–8

Succulents, compost 17, 25
  cuttings 58–60
  definition of 9
  drainage 11, 15, 25
  families of 10
  flowers of 12–14, 10
  general culture 25–28
  heating 27
  in the house 26, 146–8
  leaf cuttings 61
  offsets 61–2
Succulents, propagation of 52–7, 58–63, 144–5
  selection of 44–8
  situation 9
  special pots 28
  staking of 27–8
  transplanting 49–51
  ventilation 27, 11
  watering 26–7
Summer Cloud 25

Thrips 68
Transplanting methods 49–51, 55–6
  seedlings 55–6
  time 49–50

Vine Weevil 68

Watering 19–22, 26–7, 144–5
Woodlice 68–9

Index of Latin names

Main entries appear first

Acanthocalycium violaceum 41
Adromischus cooperi 125, 44
— maculatus 44
Aeonium arboreum atropurpureum 125, 44
— simsii 44
Agave sisalana 14
Aloe arborescens 126, 44
— aristata 126, 44
— ferox 126, 44
— variegata 125, 44

Anacampseros rufescens 127, 44
Aporocactus flagelliformis 91, 32
— mallisonii 91
Argyroderma arctophyllum 127, 44
— testiculare 127, 44
Astrophytum asterias 110
— capricorne aureum pl. 4
— myriostigma 109, 43
— — var. quadricostatum 109
— ornatum 43, 109, pl. 43

Austrocylindropuntia cylindrica 78
— — cristata 78
— salmiana 78, 32
— — albiflora 79
— subulata 79
— vestita 79
— — cristata 79
Aylostera deminuta 95, 41, pl. 10
— pseudodeminuta 95, pl. 9
— spegazziniana 95

Bergeranthus multiceps 127, 44
— scapiger 127
— vespertinus 127
Brasilicactus haselbergii 103
Brasilopuntia brasiliensis 78, 32
Bryophyllum 28

Cactanae 73
Carnegiea gigantea 88, 12, 32
Carpobrotus edulis 14
Cephalocereus palmeri 83
— senilis 32, 83, pl. 12
Cereanae 80–90, 72
Cereeae 80–124, 72
Cereus aethiops 81
— eburneus 86
— jamacaru 81
— — monstruosus 81
— peruvianus 81, 32, 53, pl. 33
— — monstruosus 81, pl. 3
— — — minor 81
— treleasei 86
Ceropegia woodii 127, 44
Chamaecereus silvestrii 13, 41, pl. 40
— — luteus 41
Cheiridopsis 27
Cleistocactus baumannii 89
— straussii 89, 32, pl. 40
Conophytum 27
— albescens 128
— bilobum 128
— minutum 128, 45
— obcordellum 128
— velutinum 45
Coryphanthanae 112–121, 73
Coryphantha clava 113
— pallida 112
— radians 112
Cotyledon undulata 128, 45
Crassula 28
— arborescens 128, 45
— falcata 129, 45
— lycopodoides 129, 45
— multicaria 61
— perforata 129, 45
— portulacea 129
— schmidtii 130, 45
— socialis 130, 45
Cyanotis somaliensis 130, 45
Cylindropuntia kleiniae 80
— leptocaulis 79
— tunicata 79

Dactylopsis 27
Dinteranthus 26
Disocactus 73
Dolicothele longimamma 44

Echeveria carnicolor 131
— derenbergii 131, 45
— gibbiflora 131, 45
— — carunculata 131
— — metallica 131, 45
— glauca 131
— harmsii 139, 46
— leucotricha 131
— multicaulis 132
— nodulosa 132
— pulvinata 132
— setosa 132
Echidnopsis cereiformis 132, 45
Echinocactanae 97–112, 73
Echinocactus grusonii 109, 43, pl. 45
— ingens 108
Echinocereanae 92–7, 72
Echinocereus 12
Echinocereus enneacanthus 93
— fitchii 93, 41, pl. 8
— pentalophus 93
— procumbens 93
— rigidissimus 93
— salm-dyckianus 92
— stramineus 93, 41
— tuberosus senilis 86
— viridiflorus 92
Echinofossulocactus hastatus 111
— lancifer 111, 44
— zacatecasensis 111, 43
Echinomastus macdowellii 112
Echinopsis 12
— eyriesii 97
— kratochvilleana 96
— multiplex 96, 32
— rhodotricha 97, 32
Epiphyllanae 121–3, 73
Epiphyllum "Ackermannii" 122
— "Cooperi" 122
— "Elegantissimum" 122, 44
Eriocactus leninghaussii 104
Espostoa lanata 83, 32
— — nana 84
Eulychnia floresii 85, 32
— iquiquensis 85
Euphorbia canariensis 9
— caput-medusae 133, 45

Euphorbia (*cont'd*)
— dregeana 14
— grandicornis 133
— hamata 13
— hermentiana 135, 133
— ingens 133
— mammillaris 134
— meloformis 134, 45
— millii 134, 46
— — "Aalbaeumle" 134
— — var. Splendens 134, 46
— — "Tananarive" 135, 46
— obesa 135, 45
— resinifera 135
— splendens var. Bojeri 134
— — prostrata 134
— submammillaris 135, 45
— trigona 133, 45, 135
— valida 135, 45

Faucaria tigrina 136, 46
— tuberculosa 136
Ferocactus 30
— corniger 110
— electracanthus 43, pl. 7
— latispinus 110
— viridescens 110
— wislizenii 110, 43
Fochea damarana 14

Gasteria 28
Gymnocalycium baldianum 10
— bruchii 105, 43
— damsii 104, 13, 42, pl. 11
— denudatum 107
— gibbosum 107
— lafaldense 105
— mihanovichii 105, 43
— — "Hibotan" 105, 43, pl. 4
— — rubrum pl. 42
— multiflorum 107
— quehlianum 108, 13, 42, pl.
— saglione 107, pl. 6
Gymnocalycium venturianum
pl. 12

Hamatocactus hamatacanthus
— setispinus 111, 43
Hariota salicornioides 123
Hatiora salicornioides 123
Haworthia cuspidata 136, 46
— papillosa 137, 46
— reinwardtii 136

Index

porus mallisonii 91
ithii 91
 carnosa 137, 46
variegata 137, 46
cereanae 90–2, 73
cereus trigonus 90
datus 91, 32

nchoe 28
harensis 137, 46
ossfeldiana 137, 46
igremontiana 137, 46
dtschenkoi marginata 46
biflora 138, 46
ia articulata 142
apeliaeformis 142

oranthus aurantiacus 46
reus 138
aireocereus aragonii 85
iseus 86
arginatus 86
gemmatus 86
uinosus 85
urberi 85
leasei 86
ps 139, 28, 46
lla 139
mptonii 139
niana 139
leri 139
rasmontana 139
liei 139
arthae 139
ckbergensis 139
vacea 139
eudotruncatella 139
ndausensis 139
ia aurea 96, 41
nsispina 95, 41
natimensis 95, 41
cristata pl. 5
oiana 96
ocereus schottii 89, 32
ophora williamsii 13

ocarpus erinaceus 101, 42
millaria aurihamata 117, pl. 14
casana 116, 13, 60, pl. 19
gotensis 118
mbycina 118
nptotricha 116, 43

Mammillaria(cont'd)
— celsiana 119
— centricirrha 120, 43
— collinsii 120
— columbiana var. bogotensis 118
— compressa 121
— decipiens 115
— elongata 114
— erythrosperma 117
— gigantea 121
— hahniana 120
— heeriana 43
— heyderi 120, 43
— kewensis 119, 13, 43
— klissingiana 119
— kunzeana 117
— lanata 120
— microhelia 114, pl. 46
— microheliopsis 115
— mundtii 119
— nejapensis 120
— nundtii 119
— parkinsonii 120
— plumosa 115
— prolifera 115, 13
— — var. texana 115
— pygmaea 118
— rhodantha 118, pl. 17
— schelhasei 116, 43
— schiedeana 115
— spinosissima 118
— uncinata 121, pl. 18
— wildii 117, 43
— woodsii 43
— zeilmanniana 116, 43, pl. 20
— — alba 116, 43, pl. 19
Marginatocereus marginatus 86
— — gemmatus 86
Marshallocereus aragonii 85
— thurberi 85
Matucana aurantiaca 41
Mediolobivia pygmaea 95, 41, pl. 21
Melocactus 73
Monvillea haagei 81, pl. 47
Myrtillocactus 13
— geometrizans 89, 32
— schenkii 90

Nananthus 27, 28
Neobuxbaumia polylopha 90, pl. 38
Neoporteria subgibbosa 108
— villosa 108

Nopalea coccinellifera 78
Nopalxochia phyllanthoides var.
   Deutsche Kaiserin 123, 44
Notocactus apricus 102, 42
— concinnus 102, 13, 42
— haselbergii 103
— horstii 103, 42
— juncineus 103, 42
— leninghaussii 104, 42
— mammulosus 101
— muricatus 102, 42
— ottonis 104, 42
— — var. linkii 104
— scopa 103, 42
— submammulosus 101, 42
— — var. pampeanus 102, 42
Nyctocereus serpentinus 86

Oliveranthus elegans 139, 46
Opuntia 12, pl. 36
— aurantiaca 75
— basilaris 75
— bergeriana 75
— brasiliensis 78
— cylindrica 78
— — cristata 78
— dillenii 76
— engelmannii 76
— extensa 75
— ficus-indica 76, 13
— horrida 76
— kleiniae 80
— leptocaulis 79
— leucotricha 76, pl. 35
— microdasys 76, 32
— — albispina 77
— — rufida 77
— — — minor 77
— monacantha 77
— — variegata 77
— x puberula 77
— robusta 77
— rufida minor 77
— salmiana 78, 32
— — albiflora 79
— spinosissima 58
— subulata 79
— tuna 77
— tunicata 79
— vestita 79
— — cristata 79
— vulgaris 78

Opuntieae 75–80, 72
Oreocereus celsianus 88, 32, 39
— fossulatus 88
Orostachys spinosus 139, 46

Pachycereus
— pecten aboriginum 84
— pringlei 84
Pachyphytum amethystinum 140
Parodia aureispina 100, 41
— aurihamata 101, 41
— chrysacanthion 41, 98, pl. 26
— gracilis 100, 42, pl. 24
— maassii 99
— mairanana 99
— microsperma 98, 42, pl. 25
— mutabilis 100, 42
— nivosa 98
— rubellihamata 99, 42
— rubriflora 100, 42
— sanagasta 99
— sanguiniflora 100, 41, pl. 23
— scopaoides 99
Pereskia aculeata 74
— — rubescens 74, 30
— godseffiana 74
— grandifolia 74, 30
Pereskieae 74, 72
Pilosocereus palmeri 83
Pleiospilos bolusii 140, 47
Pseudolobivia aurea 96, 41
— kratochvilleana 96, 32, pl. 23
Pterocactus kuntzii 80
— tuberosus 80

Rebutia 94, pls. 31 and 32
— haagei 95, 41
— marsoneri 41
— minuscula 94, 13, 41
— pygmaea 95, pl. 21
— senilis 94, 41
— — stuemeriana 94
— violaciflora 94, 41
Rhipsalidanae 123–4, 73
Rhipsalidopsis rosea 123, pl. 29
Rhipsalidopsis rosea x Schlumbergera gaertneri 123, 44, pl. 30
Rhipsalis houlletiana 124
— paradoxa 124
Rhombophyllum rhomboideum 140, 47
— nellii 140, 47
Ritterocereus pruinosus 85
Rochea falcata 129

Sanseveria trifasciata "Laurentii" 141, 47
Schlumbergera gaertneri 122, 44
— — x Rhipsalidopsis rosea 122, 44, pl. 30
Sedum lineare variegatum 141, 47
— morganianum 141
— pachyphyllum 141, 47
— sieboldii medio-variegatum 142, 47
Selenicereus boeckmannii 91, 32
— grandiflorus 91, 32
Sempervivum 142, 47
Senecio articulatus var. globosus 142, 47

Senecio (*cont'd*)
— macroglossus variegatus 14?
— stapeliaeformis 142
Setiechinopsis mirabilis 97, pl.
Stapelia 12, 47
— grandiflora 143
— variegata 143, 47
Stenocactus hastatus 111
— lancifer 111, pl. 44
— zacatecasensis 111
Stenocereus treleasei 86
Stetsonia coryne 84, 32, pl. 41

Testudinaria 14
Thelocactus bicolor 87, 32
— bicolor tricolor 113
Tradescantia navicularis 143, 4
Trichocereus chiloensis 87
— pasacana 87, 32
— santiaguensis 87
— spachianus 87, 32
— werdemannianus 87

Wigginsia erinaceus 101, 42
Wilcoxia schmollii 86

Yucca 144, 47
— filamentosa 48
— gloriosa 48

Zygocactus truncatus 122, 13,
— — "Weihnachtsfreude" 122
— — "Margrit Koeniger" 122